On Higher Ground

A Journey to Faith

Selected titles by John A. Torres

Meet our New Student from Haiti
Meet our New Student from Nicaragua
Vince Carter: Slam Dunk Artist
Hurricane Katrina 2005
Sports Great Oscar de la Hoya
The Texas Fight for Independence: From the Alamo to San Jacinto
Disaster in the Indian Ocean: Tsunami 2004
Cherokee Trail of Tears and the Forced March of a People
Sports Great Tim Duncan

On Higher Ground

A Journey to Faith

John A. Torres

NEPPERHAN PRESS, LLC
YONKERS, NY

Copyright © John A. Torres, 2010

All rights reserved. No part of this book may be reproduced or transmitted in any form or by any means, electronic or mechanical, including photocopying, recording, or by any information storage and retrieval system, without written permission from the author, except for the inclusion of brief quotations in a review.

Published by Nepperhan Press, LLC
P.O. Box 1448, Yonkers, NY 10702
nepperhan@optonline.net
nepperhan.com

Printed in the United States of America

Library of Congress Control Number: 2010933211

ISBN 978-0-9794579-9-9

Cover photo by Craig Rubadoux

DEDICATION

This very personal account of my life has been both challenging and rewarding to write. It is dedicated to the people whose love, patience, and support helped shape the person I am today: my wonderful and loving parents, my children who are my joy, Joe Hurston, who was essential in getting me on the right path, Father Page and the Holy Name of Jesus community, my beautiful and supportive wife, Jennifer, on whom I rely for everything and for the judge, who was able to recognize that the tapping on his shoulder came from God.

FOREWORD

JOHN A. TORRES is an award-winning journalist who inspires people not only by his words, but also by the life he lives. That is to say he is authentic, ruthlessly honest, and a totally credible 45-year-old human being. His success in overcoming his dysfunctional family upbringing and dissolate young adulthood offers a magnificent pattern of hope to the young and old, who are searching for meaning, purpose, and happiness in life.

Born into a Puerto Rican family, John was reared in high crime, drug-infested sections of Manhattan and the Bronx. Yet, instead of cynicism or condemnation, John shows nothing but love and compassion for his parents and family.

Despite his Catholic upbringing and education in Catholic high schools and college, John was sacramentalized, but not evangelized. This is the tragic story of so many of our young people today who may have received the Holy Spirit, but never experienced His presence or power. While Catholic education generally makes significant differences in young people's lives, it seems to fail miserably in making them committed Christians.

Like so many modern young adults, John was a confused "nominal, inactive Catholic" whose life of materialism and pleasure left him empty, unhappy, and turned off with life.

Today, John is a joy-filled, Christ-centered Catholic, a happy family man and a successful journalist, playwright, and author. His burning desire to bring Christ's love and healing to others has led him as a journalist and missionary to such desperately needy places as Haiti, Central America, and Africa.

What brought about such a dramatic change in John's life is

what *On Higher Ground* is all about. It's a book that not only makes for an interesting and fascinating read, but also one that will make a significant difference in your life. I wholeheartedly recommend this little, captivating gem of a narrative, focused on what can give meaning and purpose to your life.

>David P. Page
>Retired Editor of *The Florida Catholic*
>Retired Pastor of Holy Name of Jesus Catholic Church

ONE

IT WAS A GORGEOUS morning.

The roosters had been heralding the dawn since about 4 a.m. and when I realized that I couldn't adequately muffle their wakeup calls by wrapping my rolled-up jeans over my ears, I got dressed to go watch the sun rise over the lake.

It had been a restless night of sleep anyhow and getting up seemed all right. The barrage of thoughts racing through my mind had not been conducive to slumber. I was dealing with emotions that reached down to my core. And, of course, the constant yelping by the jackals in the distance caused more tossing and turning than I care to remember. That was one sound I just could not get used to, though I guess I should have been relieved they weren't lions.

The air was cold outside my tent and I pulled my wool Juventus soccer cap over my head, grabbed my video camera, and made my way through the predawn darkness. I walked down slowly toward the muddy banks past the tall, skinny trees that I initially mistook for Masai warriors a few days earlier and found a sturdy enough rock to climb up. From there I let the darkness dissipate and the sun's first rays kiss my face.

The heat and light from that bright wonderful star never felt so good on my face, even for an avid beachgoer like me—a transplanted New Yorker living in Florida.

As the first flashes of red and orange started creeping up over the endless horizon, my first instinct was to start videotaping this wonderful moment—my first sunrise in Africa. There was no breeze and the water on the lake was pure glass; not a single droplet was moving. It would have made for some spectacular video. But it was so quiet, so calm, and so perfect that I decided not to.

This sunrise was for me. I wouldn't be sharing this moment with anyone.

I stood there for a good thirty minutes, listening as the world slowly roused from its slumber and came alive around me. Our base camp started stirring as people woke and got ready for a day of construction around the camp. The birds and frogs started their back-and-forth songs and the goats could safely bleat without fear of the jackals, even as the roosters grew tired of their own cries.

The wonderful blending of different aromas filled the air: coffee with chicory, several types of wood burning in camp fires, the goats, chickens, and even the red clay beneath our feet. It was more than the casual witness of another day, something akin to some magical metamorphosis, like a monarch emerging from its cocooned captivity.

I continued standing still trying to make the moment last for as long as I could before reality would disturb it. For that brief period I belonged to the world and I didn't want the feeling to end. It was as if I had stowed away unnoticed and became part of this beautiful song that I knew would end before I wanted it to.

I climbed up on higher ground to get closer to the sun, stretching my neck out, as the moment's magic began to wane.

Satisfied with the small reward I had just allowed myself to have, I climbed down off the rocks, took in a deep clean breath of still-cold morning air, and went to the makeshift kitchen, which jutted up against the remnants of what had been a ten-foot-high ant hill. I poured myself a tin cup full of coffee with chicory, my new favorite morning beverage. It was hot and I liked the bitterness of it and took it black with no sugar.

I started thinking about the previous night and how now it seemed like some far away dream. My eyes felt red and swollen.

That's when I spotted someone or something coming toward our camp, not from the trail but from the thickest part of the bush. I hadn't been too concerned with security or safety in our camp until I found where we were on a map and realized we were within walking distance from the Democratic Republic of Congo, where civil war and violence was routinely spilling over the border.

We were so remote that many of these people here in the bush had never visited any of the bigger cities, ridden in a car, or had any connection to a government at all. These were people who existed outside of the government's knowledge. They were born, lived, and died without records.

But as I looked closer, rubbing my eyes for focus, I could see this wasn't a guerrilla fighter or rebel soldier. No, it was just an old man. But this old man couldn't have looked more pathetic if he tried and he probably could not have startled me more either.

He emerged slowly, barely able to walk, from the six-foot-high yellow elephant grass that encircled the deep forest, using a piece of twisted metal for a walking stick. He was ancient and his clothes were too. His sneakers had more holes than rubber on their soles and you could see his bruised feet as they stuck out from the holes in his sneakers stained with dry blood; his brown jacket was weathered and stained. His skin was full of blotches and there were dark circles of pain around his eyes. Most of his teeth had rotted out.

His body looked broken, bent in half, and seemingly not able to straighten itself upright again. It was as if he was suffering from every possible malady or malfunction the human body would allow without shutting down for good.

I stood there alone with my small tin cup of coffee, the sleep long gone from my eyes, when he appeared looking more like an apparition than a man as he slunk closer. Not knowing what to do I tried to look away—hoping he would be discouraged by my aloofness and approach someone else in the camp.

How many men like this had I walked right past without a second glance during my days in New York? This man was no different. He was just another beggar, another drunk, another homeless man looking for a handout or freebie. The only difference was that this man came out of a forest instead of a back alley or subway platform. They were all the same, right?

"Please let him keep going," I pleaded to myself. "Keep right on walking."

Even though my back was now facing him, I could feel him zeroing in on me, floating toward me with each passing second.

When he was so close that I could no longer ignore him, I turned and looked into his sad yellowing eyes that indicated malaria, and something touched me inside. He gave the universal sign of hunger—moving his empty hand to his mouth over and over, and the feeble way his shaking hands moved awoke pity in me.

What was wrong with me? My disgust was giving way to mercy. I looked around for Richard, my interpreter, or anyone really. We were not supposed to give our personal food out. And I've been in enough third-world countries to know that you don't just start handing out food. It can get dangerous, especially if others show up demanding food and you have nothing left to give. Desperate people are capable of dangerous actions. Plus there was a process for the hungry to receive food here at the Teen Missions Rescue Center located in Solwezi, Zambia just a few clicks from the Congo border. Wandering unannounced into camp and motioning your hand to your mouth was not part of the process.

But what could I do? He was not going away and clearly he needed help, my help. My eyes darted around the camp once again looking for someone to intervene. It was as if the old man and I existed on some other plane and no one could see us. When it was clear no one was coming to my rescue, I gave him the universal sign for wait right here, holding my palm up followed by only my index finger. I ran to my tent wondering why it was so difficult for me to offer this man help, knowing full well that I would have no problem feeding a stray dog who wandered into camp.

I moved quickly, worried that the old man would be gone by the time I returned, and pulled out a few peanut butter protein bars and two packages of tuna in lemon pepper sauce.

And there they were. There, still lying on my sleeping bag were the scraps of paper from the night before. I ran my hand over them lightly touching them and for a moment I lost my breath. I picked one up and smiled thinking about where I was ten hours earlier.

This crazy ragtag bunch of Christian American teenagers, misfits most of them, had spent the hours after supper sitting by the canteen area in the glow of a solitary light bulb powered by our truck. They had just finished devotions and some of the girls had even sung a contemporary Christian song called "God of Wonders" that had morphed into an earworm and was burrowing into my brain pleading with me to hum it.

They then started a bonding exercise as I took notes for the series of articles I would be writing about them upon returning to the states. The idea was simple: They each were given a slip of paper with their name written on top. The papers were passed out to the group and they took turns writing something positive about the person whose name was on top.

It had been a long day and I was thankful the exercise did not involve puppets or songs or fire and brimstone sermons. It was done nearly in silence while we sat on the dusty stairs carved into the red clay earth.

I was loving Africa but I was starting to really miss my wife and children back home and also desperately missing my daily fix of Major League Baseball. I don't think I had ever gone so long without knowing how my beloved New York Mets were faring. The pennant race was heating up before I left and I was hopeful they would still be leading the Phillies by the time I returned to the states.

Africa was a great assignment and I could feel jealousy from my fellow reporters at *Florida Today* newspaper where I worked.

This opportunity was both rewarding and challenging for someone like me. I was able to climb through the window of a world I could never belong to for a prolonged glimpse. I was able to embed myself with people that had true faith in God.

I loved God. I believed that Jesus Christ was His only son and that He was sent down to save us from sin. I really did believe those things. But I didn't believe them like these kids did. They believed it and they lived it. They were living it right now, washing the feet of total strangers and caring for them. The best I could muster was to write about them and their faith.

Yeah, I was good with words all right, but actions were a different story.

These kids spent the year saving money and holding fundraisers in order to raise the $3,000 plus it took to get them to Africa for five weeks on their mission of mercy. They traveled thousands of miles with little more than the clothes on their backs in order to each tote 70 pounds worth of socks and shoes to the continent that was being decimated by a deadly disease, AIDS.

Their mission was one of simple beauty and service. They were to wash the feet of as many AIDS orphans—children whose parents succumbed to the disease—and then put socks and shoes on their feet. Many of the children had contracted the disease as well and would die without ever being diagnosed. For the majority, it would be the first pair of shoes they ever owned.

Their faith was astounding and I was slightly jealous. One of the American teens said his parents offered him an all-expense-paid trip to Europe only if he wouldn't go on the mission trip. Another said he chose the trip instead of a Hawaiian vacation with his family.

Europe? Hawaii? I didn't get it. But I knew that if I had any chance at writing the story the right way I would have to understand why anyone would chose to humble himself and wash a stranger's feet instead of taking some magnificent vacation anywhere else.

Many of the AIDS orphans had infected feet or open sores that had to be treated before they could get their shoes. It was a job that I personally wouldn't have done for pay and here were teens that actually paid money for a chance to wash a poor child's feet.

If I considered myself to be a Christian then it would have to be the equivalent of light beer, while these teens were like God's soldiers on steroids and they weren't afraid or embarrassed to show it.

I remember one of them, Tobi from California, asked me one day if I was a Christian and I wasn't sure how to respond.

"Of course I am. I'm a Catholic," I wanted to say but couldn't force the words from my mouth. He had unknowingly unmasked me and I had no real answer for him. It was at that instant, that moment he asked me if I was a Christian, that I realized I was not. I knew I wasn't a Christian, not in the true sense and certainly not like he was.

Maybe I had been raised in the Catholic Church but I couldn't really call myself a Catholic, not a practicing one anyway.

"Sort of," I managed with nary a smattering of conviction. "I guess I'm a Catholic."

Tobi gave me a funny, polite smile like he didn't understand but wanted to. To his credit he sensed that my comfort level had deteriorated and let the conversation drift away. Talking about God was something I just didn't do.

I found myself humming "God of Wonders" in my head while hoping they would be done with the exercise soon so I could get to sleep. Tomorrow would be a big day as my photographer and I had arranged to attend the funeral of a 35-year-old mother who had died of AIDS. That would be the final missing piece in our story and I was excited to get it over and done with.

I would be going home the day after that and I was feeling a bit worn out.

Except for a few giggles, the evening breeze rustling through the elephant grass, and the yelping jackals in the distance, it was quiet in camp. The interpreters were down near the banks of the lake huddled around a small campfire that glowed more than it flickered. I could hear them talking about how the country was in need of a revolution. What a great spot to enjoy a cocktail, I thought.

When the American teens were finally done with what seemed an unnecessarily long exercise, I noticed that many of them were looking at me and smiling. My stomach took on an immediate uneasy feeling.

Tobi handed me three small slips of paper that had my name written on it.

They had included me in the exercise.

I took the papers and had barely started to read when I could feel my insides tremble and convulse from the struggle to hold back tears. I felt the wind leave my lungs and my head go light.

"Thank you for loving these kids enough to come out here. God is really working here," one wrote.

"You are awesome," another said.

"I miss you already."

"You are truly a man of God."

"God will not forget what you did here for these kids."

I clutched the papers in my fist and wept. I knew these things were not true. How could they be? I was a sinner, a phony. They didn't know me. If they knew what I was really like they would have left the sheets of paper blank. They didn't know it, but I knew there was no way God could love me the way He loved them.

I was just another cynical newspaper man looking to make a name for himself. Why didn't they see what I did? Why did they see these things? Why would God cloud their judgment so much?

One by one they lined up and hugged me as I continued to cry.

"Good night John. It's OK to let go. It's OK to cry."

"It's clear just how much you love these children that are suffering. Thanks for coming here to write about them. Your words, your articles will save lives."

I said goodnight through the steady stream of tears that formed little canyons on my face through the dust that had settled on my skin all day long. I walked back to my tent silently not knowing what to feel, reduced to a sniffling mess. It's one thing to hear accolades from those who love you, family and friends. But never had I experienced nor expected anything like this.

I lay on my back and the warm tears continued to well in my eyes before rolling down the sides of my face. I turned on my flashlight and read the notes over and over again until I drifted off to peaceful sleep with the glow of my flashlight painting the inside of my tent with a yellow hue.

I picked up one of the notes and smiled before putting it back down carefully and leaving my tent with the food for the old man. I also made sure to bring my Sony digital video camera, the one I refused to click on at the sunrise. I scrambled back out of my tent and ran back down toward the old man. Richard, to my great relief, was there talking with him. I held out the food and the old man took it without looking at what I was giving him.

He nodded at me. Richard gave me a quick smile.

"He is hungry," Richard said in thickly accented English. "He says he has nothing to eat."

"What was he doing in the woods?" I asked, while clumsily putting a tiny videotape into the camera. "Is that where he lives? Does he have a camp in there?"

Richard shook his head no, searching for the right words.

"Ah, how do you say? He was foraging. He was looking for food." With that, Richard make a scratching motion with his hands, as if to say the man had literally been on his hands and knees digging for some morsel that could count as food.

My God, I thought, this old man needs to look for food in

this dried-up forest every day? Then I thought of the homeless elsewhere. The dozens, hundreds, I passed by without a second thought every year. They were really no different. They foraged for food in dumpsters and soup kitchens. But this seemed even more pitiful. There were no soup kitchens or shelters to turn to here. There was no food in these woods, especially now in the dry season. Any game had long been killed and eaten.

In fact, earlier that week I observed a young mother holding one child in her arms and another in a papoose on her back kneeling in the water.

For hours she knelt in the water constantly checking something in her hand. Overcome with curiosity I walked down to the lake hoping my photographer and I would not frighten her away.

What I finally saw was an image that will probably stay forever etched in my heart. This poor woman was using an old coca-cola glass bottle to try and catch minnows so that her children would have something to eat, a little protein for the soup she was making later that day.

I took a closer look and saw that she had put a tiny bit of cornmeal in the bottle and then would hold it under water to attract the tiny little fish. The minnows that would be supper for her family were much smaller than the minnows I would ever consider using for bait. If it hadn't been so sad, it would have been funny. She was quite proud of herself, holding up the bottle to show us her prized catch and I'm sure that the fish would keep her children alive, for now.

She loved her children so much, I'm sure she would have stayed out there all day long if she had to.

It was just another of numerous eye-opening moments that week that really made me think twice before complaining about minor things like not finding something to watch on my 250 cable television channels or being forced to wait in long lines at the supermarket when I'm buying only one item or the inevitable cloudy weather I encounter whenever I plan a day at the beach.

One little girl that week wanted to put her brand new shoes that she had just received in the offertory after a church service. Another child took his shoes off immediately and carried them in his arms for the rest of the day because he didn't want to get them dirty.

I also visited a 30-year-old woman who was lying down by a fire waiting to die. Suffering from both malaria and AIDS, she was sick with worry about the fate of her children. She was careful not to use the word AIDS, merely calling it the sickness. Her kids would have it hard enough without the bad luck and stigma that comes from a mother who died of AIDS.

They likely would end up staying in their tiny village, sleeping outdoors or with the animals. No one would pay their school fees and certainly no one would adopt them. Would there be anyone to love them? Would anyone catch minnows in the pond for them?

Then there was the day my photographer and I went on a walk with the interpreter, Richard, and we stumbled upon a makeshift cemetery in the middle of the woods. There was no rhyme or reason as to why it was where it was. The only thing I could think of was that people wanted it to remain a quiet secret. Most of the grave markers were beneath several inches of fallen leaves and we wouldn't have even found it had it not been for a few freshly dug graves. A closer look at the wooden crosses and markers was stark evidence at how AIDS was ravaging sub-Saharan Africa and not only in big cities but out here in rural areas as well.

There was not one single person over the age of 40 buried there. Most of the people were in their 20s and 30s including several young children. Along with the markers or small crosses were plastic flowers, religious symbols as well as bowls and cups owned by the deceased.

Richard explained that in some cultures it is an honor to be buried with your cup or bowl. But this, he said was different.

This display was about people afraid of catching the disease and wanting to get rid of the dead person's belongings.

Not all the things we learned that week were sad, though they were all devastating. But even a disturbing story could have a happy ending. We visited a dormitory for young teenage girls built on the grounds of the secondary school they were attending. Because the secondary schools are so few and far between, most kids are forced to drop out of school after a basic elementary education. Those girls who wanted to further their education usually had to travel great distances to go to school. They would try and find homes that would take them in as boarders. In exchange for a place to stay, they would help out around the house and even help raise other children. But many times the men in the homes would take advantage of the situation.

The bottom line was girls were getting raped. Many became pregnant and several others contracted AIDS and their dreams of going to school and having a career were dashed. The first dormitory that was built had 20 beds and more than 40 girls initially signed up. By the end of the first year there were 67 girls and another unit was built.

Happy ending? Well, the headmaster of the school told us that before the dormitories were built, 50 percent of his female students became pregnant or contracted AIDS. That number dropped to zero after the girls had a safe place to stay.

But it was hard imagining a happy outcome for this ragged old man that wandered into camp begging for food. There seemed no way that he could fend for himself. This old man was so broken down that there was no way he could even try to catch minnows for dinner without plopping over and drowning. I wondered how long it had been since he last ate. I wondered how much longer he had to live.

I began to videotape. I asked Richard to find out who this man was and what caused him to end up like this. All this poor man wanted was food and I felt the need to interview him first!

Well, I reasoned right back to myself that I wasn't the one who was there on the mission trip. I was there to write a story for my newspaper and help produce a few short Internet videos to go along with it. That—not feeding this man—was my responsibility. The missionaries were there to save lives. I was merely there to write about it.

I didn't think of the torment and the criticism Pulitzer-winning photographer Kevin Carter went through after snapping a photo of a crumpled, starving Sudanese girl with a vulture standing close by. He reportedly scared away the vulture after taking the shot, yet people were critical of him to the point that it drove him to deep depression. Shortly after receiving the highest honor there was in his field, Carter—still haunted by the images and backlash—killed himself.

No, I didn't think of him at all.

I wanted my interview.

I started asking my questions. The man's name was Benson Kapoma. He was 88 years old and all seven of his children had died of AIDS.

"I have no one left," he said through Richard. "I have no one to take care of me. At my age I thought I would be living with one of my children. But there is no one left. It is all because of AIDS."

Both his voice and spirit seemed broken and his words resembled more of a cry than a language anyone could understand. I felt a pit in my stomach.

"AIDS has destroyed my country," he continued. "Something needs to be done. There needs to be a change in this country or else more and more people will continue to suffer."

It dawned on me that like the hundreds of African children I had encountered that week, he was an AIDS orphan now as well. Imagine an 88-year-old man forced to gather food in the woods every day. My heart became sick with compassion for this man. I thought of my own father and mother, who are blessed with good health and happiness in their 70s. I imagined my dad wearing these tattered rags and leaning over a scrap-metal cane and it made me want to cry.

I knelt down to get a better angle with the camera as he continued speaking with Richard. I had stopped listening and stopped asking questions. This interview was over even though the camera continued to record. I only felt sorrow for this man and wished I had given him all of my power bars and tuna and not just some of it. I noticed how tightly his weak hands clutched the power bars as he continued talking in his weepy language.

The roosters had long stopped crying and the chickens were chasing each other all over the compound. I was feeling sleepy from having woken before the sun did. I couldn't wait to get back to the canteen for another cup of coffee.

Now that same sun was nearly completely risen behind him and there was glare on the viewfinder. I moved slightly to one side for a clearer picture and I saw something else entirely. It was right there on my screen. I gasped and tears quickly washed the dust from my already puffy eyes.

Benson Kapoma was no longer the ragged old man in ratty clothes. Instead, I saw Jesus Christ, regaled in red and white robes in all His glory. He looked at me in a gentle, majestic, loving way and I could say nothing. I stared, holding my breath for several moments and then the image was gone.

The old man eventually wandered away with a bag of nuts, some cereal, and a few pieces of fruit. I watched him walk away and disappear into the forest like a slow lifting fog that merely blended in with the yellow elephant grass and brown trees.

I was sure that he would make it for at least another few days. But what about me: A tough, or so I thought, ex-New Yorker, former carpenter who was now an award-winning reporter for a major daily newspaper. Would I be all right? What exactly had I seen?

I tried telling myself that I could not have seen what I did.

For the rest of the day and night I thought of the old man and of Jesus, the son of God. How could I not have? Something inside me wished I had followed him into the forest. I wished that I had the courage to give him all my food instead of just some extra items I had. I wished I had the faith to bend down and wash his feet and put a pair of shoes on him.

I wished I cared for more than just my story while I was talking with him. Instead of looking for that killer quote that would help my story win some press award, I wished I had truly listened to him.

Even a borderline believer like me knew about Matthew 25:40, "Whatsoever you do to the least of my brothers, you have done unto me." Sure, even Catholics like me who would grace a church with my presence only on Easter and Christmas knew that verse. Plus, I remembered it from the church hymn back in my altar boy days.

While I had always gotten a certain sense of comfort from that verse, now it was filling me with dread. I sure was hoping that wasn't the case. After all, how many times had I done the wrong thing to—or simply ignored—the least of my brothers? I was great at trampling on feelings and relationships, acting selfishly without any regard for others or for consequences.

How many times had I walked right past the least of my brothers and done nothing?

Knowing that there was no way on God's green earth that Jesus would ever show Himself to a worthless unrepentant sinner like me, I doubted what I had seen. Yet the image of Jesus, glorious and victorious, was there every time I closed my eyes.

I told no one of what I had seen that day until I returned home to my wife a few days later. I could not erase the image or memory from my mind, no matter how hard I tried to rationalize that it could not have happened.

I was merely caught up in the excitement and the fervor of being with all these teenaged missionaries. Perhaps their words the night before on the wonderful notes they gave me were what caused the image to pop into my head.

But at the same time, I knew I had seen something.

I didn't want to be one of those people, the type who sees Jesus in their French toast or the Virgin Mary on the side of a building.

No, it couldn't have happened. I didn't know what it meant anyhow. But it would be the start of everything for me.

TWO

I WAS BORN John Albert Torres on August 18, 1965 in the high-crime, drug-infested area of Washington Heights in upper Manhattan. I remember graffiti and the strong smell of urine from under the stairwell but not much else, as I had barely turned five when my father moved the family to a gigantic new apartment complex that opened in the northeast Bronx known as Co-op City.

This was the country for us city dwellers and the Promised Land for those of us in middle to lower-middle class families. It was a step above the housing projects and people from different races and backgrounds flocked to Co-op City like a modern day Ellis Island. For many it was a place for second chances.

Co-op City was built on a swampy area that had once been home to the Freedom Land amusement park. On hikes with my dad we sometimes found old ride tickets that had somehow survived the years. Because it was built on a swamp, some of the land surrounding the buildings eventually began to sink.

My dad would sometimes laugh about how he considered the Bronx to be "upstate" when he was growing up in Spanish Harlem.

There were 35 buildings, each at least 24 stories high, and the complex had its own power plant, security force, playgrounds, schools, baseball fields, and shopping centers. It was a wonderful place to grow up considering it looked like a cold Orwellian city neighborhood. I always felt safe and I had lots of good friends who didn't make fun of my stutter.

In addition to mom, dad, and my two sisters, there was also plenty of extended family around as aunts, uncles, cousins, and even my grandmother moved into the sprawling apartment complex.

I was a cradle Catholic, as my father and mother were before me. Going to church on Sunday mornings wasn't optional nor a burden just a simple matter of fact. Every Sunday was the same: mom would make pancakes and sausages and after I was done eating I would sop up the leftover maple syrup on my plate with slices of mild cheddar cheese—something that always made my dad shake his head even though he joined me in dropping bits of cheese into our cups of coffee. Then we would dress and go to church. Sometimes my father would join us as well.

We belonged to St. Michael's Parish, which at that time was no more than a community room below the supermarket in one of three community centers in our new city within a city. There were no pews or kneelers. Instead, we sat on metal folding chairs, the same type my parents put out for their annual New Year's Eve bash. There was no stained glass, no statues, no baptismal font, no confessionals, no pomp or circumstance. There was a small organ and sometimes someone would even show up to play it. No, it was definitely a bare-boned low-budget operation. But it was in this church that I received the sacraments of first communion and reconciliation. Looking back now, it didn't really matter that it was missing elements that most would expect from their Catholic church.

My mother, Carmen, was born in Aguas Buenas, Puerto Rico, where she was one of 15 children to grow up on a small farm in a mountainous area about an hour's drive from San Juan. She moved to the U.S. mainland in the 1950s during the massive immigration of Puerto Ricans looking for a better life that places like New York supposedly had in store for them.

No one ever called her Carmen; they called her "Coqui" after the tiny Puerto Rican tree frogs. She often regaled my sisters and me with stories of growing up on a small farm in the kind of town where everyone knew your name and where picnics turned into town affairs. There was no television or radio and one of my mother's chores was to do laundry in the nearby stream with some of her sisters. They were very poor and she never even went to a movie theater until she started dating my father years later in New York.

She told us of the long walks to school and how boys would tease her by clamping little lizards to her earlobes in the middle of class. She told us how they would slaughter a pig and utilize just about everything the animal had to offer. I've never been able to look at blood sausage the same way. She told us how shoes and clothing got passed down from older siblings to the young ones and how one of her sisters got sick and died after being bitten by a bat.

She would laugh sadly when recounting how Santa Claus did not regularly visit the island, leaving the task of gift-giving to the Three Wise Men who every January 6, the day of the Epiphany, would leave a present under your bed in exchange for a little bit of hay they would use to feed their camels.

This kind of creeped me out.

I mean, everyone knows Santa Claus is an elf with magical powers. But the Wise Men? Where did they come from? Were they ghosts? Immortals? Worse yet, were they zombies?

Anyway it always made me sad when my mother told us the story of the year they never came.

She was a little girl when her mother told her not to put any hay in the shoebox under her bed because the Wise Men would not be giving out gifts this year. It was a rough year financially for the family—as most years were—and the daily struggle to put enough rice and beans on the table was noble enough without having to worry about gifts for all the children. My mother did not believe her. After all, the Wise Men had never let her down before.

She had faith.

So right before going to bed on January 5, she collected some hay and grass for the camels to feast on. Of course, she was heartbroken the following morning when she woke bright and early to see what treasure they had left her and found nothing but her hay.

Listening to her stories sort of brought to mind a Puerto Rican version of "Little House on the Prairie," and I found it a thrill as a 12-year-old to swim in the same creek that she had as a child and where she had washed the family's clothes. I only wish the memories were now more than yellowing photographs in my mind.

She was, and remains to this day, a religious woman. When I was a child she dutifully prayed the rosary daily and even helped start a rosary devotional every Tuesday night with her friends. Her faith in God was simple, childlike, and I enjoyed seeing her interact with God. Whenever something was misplaced in our home she petitioned St. Anthony to help us find the item and she prayed to St. Jude when something seemed hopeless.

My one complaint though was that since Spanish was her first language that was the mass we went to on Sunday afternoons.

Not only did the 12:30 p.m. mass eat into football watching time but I also understood very little about what was going on, even after I became an altar boy. Part of this had to do with my father, a native New Yorker who managed a shaver repair shop in Manhattan. Knowing and having experienced all too well the racism that exists in this world, my father insisted that his children learn to speak English before any other language. So while my older sister had no problem mastering both languages, I got stuck with English only.

I got very little out of going to church back then. Instead of concentrating on what the priest was trying to say, I merely listened for the verbal cues I learned regarding when to stand for the offertory gifts, when to fetch the water and wine, and, of course, when to get ready with my paten to catch any errant Eucharist wafers that might fall out of someone's mouth. No one really took it by hand then.

When I wasn't serving as an altar boy, my lack of understanding Spanish really made the mass boring for me.

Sometimes my younger sister, Nancy, and I would pass the time trying to make each other laugh. The hope was to give the other a case of the uncontrollable giggles. Trying to contain laughter in a place you're not supposed to be laughing always wound up being memorable. Being two years older, I usually won that game.

We played other games too. Our favorite was paper tennis where we stood on opposite sides of a bed and using a crumpled piece of paper as the ball and our hands as the racquets, played tennis. We'd laugh ourselves silly because we'd never move our feet as if we were glued to our spots.

To make matters worse for me at church, more often than not the mass was given by one of two Indian priests assigned to the parish who had a hard enough time being understood when they spoke English. Their Spanish was atrocious but the church had a hard time luring priests to this subterranean parish that must have felt like the equivalent of ice station zebra for them.

I can only imagine that it must have been the same experience for my maternal grandmother, who lived only a few apartment buildings away. She couldn't speak a lick of English yet she went to mass daily. I wondered what it was exactly that she was getting out of going. Was she making a down payment on her spot in heaven? She didn't need to. If ever I knew anyone holy, it was her.

I never saw my grandmother, whom we all called "Mamita," angry or worried. I never heard her say a bad word about anyone. And right up until she was hospitalized with the cancer that killed her at the age of 92, she cooked her own dinner every day, looked after my cousins who made Seuss's Thing One and Thing Two seem tame, walked the mile-long path around the "greenway," and went to church daily.

She praised God right up until her last breath.

She observed the Lenten fasts and all the traditional Catholic feast days but there was one day a year that she fasted completely that I found amazing. Every Thanksgiving, dozens of our family members would gather in her small apartment as she cooked, prepared, and served our holiday feast all by herself. There was turkey, pork, yellow rice with pigeon peas, pasteles, salads, and an array of snacks and cheeses.

But she ate none of it, not one morsel.

She fasted, she would explain, as a show of solidarity with the poor and suffering in this world that do not have enough to eat. What better day to do it than on the day we thank God for the bounty He has provided.

One of my many regrets is not having learned to speak Spanish properly in order to know her better on a personal level. I admired her from afar, her strength, her beauty, but never did I have a long meaningful conversation with her.

Somehow I must have made an impression on her as one of dozens of grandchildren, that she promised me the American flag that draped the casket of her husband, my grandfather, a veteran. That flag is proudly displayed in my home.

I'm sure some of my memories have been romanticized by the passage of time, but I can't picture my "Mamita" without the glow that seemed to surround her. And, at least to me, she seemed more celestial than of this world.

My dad was a Catholic as well, though I would hardly have called him traditional. He rarely went to church with us on Sundays when I was a child, choosing instead to lock himself in his bedroom most Saturday afternoons and going into deep prayer in front of a small shrine filled with at least a dozen large detailed statues of the Infant of Prague, St. Lazarus complete with wound-licking hounds, the Virgin Mary, St. Jude, and my favorite, St. Michael the Archangel, who was wielding an awesome sword about the to strike the devil himself whose grotesque, horned head was pinned beneath the archangel's sandaled foot.

Raised by an alcoholic mother and a philandering father who physically abused her, my dad was forced to find church where he could. And in the poor streets of Spanish Harlem, sometimes the lines between religion and superstition were blurred. As a young man he worked in his father's botanica shop in Spanish Harlem, a store that mixed Catholic traditions with African rituals, voodoo, and Santeria. It was the kind of store you could go in and find a beautiful crucifix, a statue of your favorite saint, remembrance candles, ingredients for a love potion, a voodoo doll, or a spray that would help you pick the lucky numbers in next week's lottery.

My father's experiences may have taught him to pray in a certain way, but all the years he spent helping my grandfather man the store and sell exotic and inexpensive cure-alls never prepared him to deal with the devils he would face later in life: a wife who started drinking too much and his own violent demons that erupted whenever he found her drunk.

I found the statues in my dad's collection to be a little scary. There seemed to be a lot of unhappy figures. But the image I was drawn to most—and the one that scared me the most—and the one I remember vividly to this day was the large crucifix hanging on the wall above their bed. It was not the glorious, risen, or even hopeful Christ. It was a graphic depiction of a man dying a slow death on a cross. It was bloody and painful even to look at.

Plain and simple, it was the son of God in anguish.

I often wondered why anyone would want that above his bed or how anyone could draw strength from that image. It would take me many years and a journey through many countries to understand this fully.

Though the image was painful, I found it hard to look away.

But even as a child, especially when serving as an altar boy during the services I didn't understand, I stared at the crucifix hanging behind the altar. I loved looking at Jesus knowing the story didn't end with His death, even if I wasn't sure I understood why He had to die.

I loved growing up in Co-op City. I had friends from just about every nationality and ethnic background. If America was the melting pot then Co-op City was the ladle stirring the mixture. There was no dominant race or group. I attended as many bar mitzvahs as I did confirmations. My friends were the children of middle-class workers, ranging from jewelers to bankers to mechanics.

Summers there were magical.

I would wait for my band of friends to ring my intercom—they had to wait until 10 a.m., which was one of mom's rules. Then, armed with baseball mitt, wooden bat, and a handful of greasy, grass-stained baseballs, we would spend all day playing pickup baseball games on a gigantic open field known as the "greenway." I remember all their names to this day: Lenny, Dave, Teddy, Chumbley, Joey, Alan, and Tommy.

The greenway was our second home. If any one of our parents wanted to find us they would look there first. It makes me sad to think that a few years ago they actually did pave over our paradise to put up a parking lot. The parking garages—already sinking slowly in the swamp—were condemned when the brickwork started falling apart, leaving no option for the thousands of families living there but to get rid of the ball fields, bandstand, and an amazing wide-open grassy field to create more parking spaces.

Short lunch breaks from our long days on the baseball diamond were spent getting a slice of pizza at Capri Pizzeria or a buttered bagel then going to the bakery where they served iced slurpee drinks in tall collectible plastic cups of our favorite baseball players. We all tried so hard to get our favorite ballplayers. I wanted a Tom Seaver plastic cup more than anything one summer only to wind up with a dozen Mike Schmidts and several Reggie Jacksons.

But that seemed to always be my luck. One summer we scored tickets to Bat Day at Yankee Stadium where all kids under the age of 12 received a full-sized wooden baseball bat with a replica signature. The Yankees were stocked with so many great players that just about every souvenir bat would be a prize.

My friends got Thurman Munson, Mickey Rivers, Graig Nettles, and Reggie Jackson. Me? I got Ron Bloomberg. I guess it wasn't as bad as another friend of mine who got Horace Clark.

We played ball until it got dark then raced home for dinner. We never had to make plans for the following day because life was a wonderful endless cycle of baseball, pizza, slurpees, and more baseball. When it got too hot, we'd find some shade and play slap ball.

Winters were different. We raced home from school, dropped off our books, and met down on the greenway to play football. Two-hand-touch was our game but when it snowed we graduated to tackle football. Mom always prepared for my return when it got dark by spreading newspaper on the floor for my wet clothes and heating up a small pot of milk for the hot cocoa. Homework was done after supper.

My parents are amazing people and were terrific as parents. My dad coached every Little League baseball team I ever played for and even if it was difficult I remember my mother being at every game. During the winter months, my dad would come home from work, grab his catcher's mitt, and take me down to the basement of our apartment building where the laundry room was and I would pitch to him. We'd get some awfully strange looks down there. Don't ask me how he was able to see the baseball in the dimly lit hallways or how he dealt with the bruised shins from my errant throws.

My parents regularly took my sisters and me to the Bronx Zoo, the Museum of Natural History, Jones Beach on Long Island, and on great vacations to Florida, Puerto Rico, and Wildwood on the Jersey shore.

My dad always packed our baseball gloves and it didn't matter if we were vacationing in San Juan or Washington, D.C. He'd always make time for us to throw the ball around. I wasn't allowed to go swimming at Jones Beach until we played catch. Of course, I wish I appreciated it then the way I do now.

And it paid off too. I was a great baseball player. And having made several all-star and competitive teams, I began to think there might be a chance I could one day play in the major leagues. I knew that was every kid's dream but I also felt that I was better than most of the kids I knew.

My mother would always get me a hot sausage with mustard and onions from the Greek lady's hot dog cart outside Montefiore Hospital every Tuesday and Thursday after my allergy shots. And I'd reciprocate by trying to scare her. I'd turn the radio up full blast right after she turned off the car when we got to the hospital. After our sausage snack she'd get in the car to start it up only to get jolted by the booming rock music on WPLJ.

Every Christmas, our tree was always loaded down with double and triple the amounts of gifts my friends received. Our parents were experts at getting every gift on our wish lists and then topping it with some totally unexpected gift that wound up being our favorite. One year it was the full collection of Tales from the Crypt horror comic books collected in a hardback anthology.

Another year my father used his contacts in Washington, D.C. to get me a framed autographed photo of my favorite football player, John Riggins.

And every year, my mother would use her own pocket money earned selling Avon products to get me a bottle of after shave splash in the shape of a classic car.

Before Christmas the family would sit together to watch any version of *A Christmas Carol* that was airing on television. Our collective favorite was unanimous. We all loved the musical version of *Scrooge* starring Albert Finney in the leading role. We had first seen that version at Radio City Music Hall back when they actually showed movies before the Christmas spectacular starring the Rockettes.

Christmas was always the best time of year. I remember going with my dad every Christmas Eve to the delicatessens and bakeries on Arthur Avenue for the spread he put out every holiday. I was proud to walk in with him and observe the rapport he had with the shopkeepers. They all seemed to know him and they'd offer him a shot of whiskey or brandy. Sometimes they gave me a sugary treat.

Then we'd drive downtown to Yorkville in Manhattan for marzipan and daisy cake. We'd finish the day in Spanish Harlem at "La Marqueta" where we'd stock up on Puerto Rican delights like chorizo, blood sausage called morcilla, queso blanco, and alcapurias. Again, everyone seemed to know my father and everywhere we went they offered him a "palito" or a shot.

If my life was perfect then, Christmas was a glimpse of paradise.

I can't pinpoint the exact moment my mother became an alcoholic or when my father started beating her.

I only remember how this beautiful, perfect life I had started crumbling all around. Our castle, it seemed, was built on sand not rock and through the cracks that formed all around light escaped and darkness crept in.

Looking back now, it's clear that my mother probably suffered from depression. Taking a farm girl who would catch lizards and swim in the creek and plopping her into this foreign life cooped up in an apartment raising three kids in the Bronx was probably not the life she dreamed of as a little girl. She must have wanted more, but to this day I don't know her dreams.

My dad was old fashioned and he never wanted her to get a job. The kids were enough work and it was the husband's responsibility to provide for the family. I can imagine that there was only so much you could do in a small apartment before the bottles of gin and vodka in my dad's liquor cabinet fooled her into having the answers.

It also didn't help that the aunts, uncles, and cousins who lived nearby were big drinkers as well and never passed up the opportunity to open a bottle of beer or pour themselves a gin with grapefruit juice. If the Irish are known as being big drinkers then the Puerto Ricans must be a very close second.

They say we repeat the patterns of our own parents and so my dad's reaction to coming home after a hard day of work to find his wife slurring words, passed out, or crying drunkenly was always the same: anger. He never tried to understand what was causing her to drink. He thought she was weak. Like his father before him, he never understood that alcoholism is a disease passed down from one generation to the next.

His lack of understanding was surprising considering that his own mother, my grandmother, killed herself with alcohol.

Having suffered a heart attack in her late 60s, she was instructed to stop drinking and smoking upon her release from the hospital. Of course she couldn't do that. Her days were spent sitting by the window of her Washington Heights tenement smoking cigarettes and drinking Budweiser. She had done that for 40 years. Nothing was going to break that habit, not even a failing ticker.

Within a week of being released from Jewish Memorial Hospital, she was dead. And I think he blamed himself for not forcing her to move into our home with us.

Her death was the only time I ever heard my father cry. Of course I had seen him tear up on other occasions, but this was different.

"My mother is gone," he yelled during the wake, spittle and tears coming together at the corners of his mouth. "Oh my God, she's gone."

I don't remember the first beating. But I remember my mother's black eyes and bruised face. I remember my mom going to church wearing sunglasses. I remember starting to fear the evenings when he would come home from work and how my heart sank to hear the jingle-jangle of his keys just outside the door. I remember the sick feeling in my stomach when I would get home from school and could immediately see that she had been drinking.

It didn't help any that my mother was such a sloppy and out of control drinker. There was no way she could hide it. Her words immediately started slurring; she became belligerent before finally getting weepy. She personally extended the cocktail hour to cocktail afternoons.

One evening my parents were hosting a dinner party for some of the executives at my dad's company. My mom was making her delicious pot roast with mashed potatoes, vegetables and salad. She started drinking too early and when it time it was to cook, she realized that she didn't have potatoes. She tried faking it with a box of instant mashed potatoes but didn't have enough flakes either.

That didn't stop her from making them anyway. By the time they were done, the mashed potatoes resembled nothing like mashed potatoes but merely a spattering of skim milk on everyone's plate.

That night there would be hell to pay.

It started becoming a bad dream, the kind you can never seem to wake up from soon enough. And it was always the same. Dad would try to beat her into sobriety. She would apologize for drinking so much. He would apologize for getting physical and things would get back to normal until the next episode. I couldn't understand why she had to keep drinking, knowing how it would wind up.

The worst incidents took place after they would get home from one of the Spanish-American club dances held at the same community center where our folding chair church was. My parents and all their friends would gather every few months and turn the center into a dance hall, where live salsa bands would blare their rhythms and pulsing beats into the early morning hours and my parents would get hammered.

There are certain memories, good or terrible, that you just never forget. Just about everyone knows exactly where they were when they first heard about the attacks on the Twin Towers. Well, my twin towers came crashing down over and over again whenever I was awakened from a deep, peaceful sleep to the sounds of my father beating my mother and her screaming.

Other than being molested, I can't think of anything worse

for a child than to be startled from a dream to face the sickening reality that his father was beating his mother. It's amazing what my sisters and I had to endure.

This cycle of dysfunction lasted many years and my stuttering grew worse. My older sister, Maryellen, couldn't deal with it and moved out the first chance she could. I think she felt bad for me and knew how much I suffered because when she moved out we started spending a lot of time together. She would take me to Jack in the Box for tacos and then to the Whitestone Drive-In theater where we would laugh and scream at the latest horror flicks.

She always made me feel special and I loved when we would go for drives. It didn't bother me in the least that the ulterior motives were really to check on a boyfriend or make sure someone saw her. I still felt older and she treated me like an adult.

I loved scary movies. I saw the *Exorcist* when I was 11. My sister, Maryellen, and I shared a love of slice-and-dice films. The more gore the better. Sometimes the images would frighten us or even disturb us and other times they would just make us laugh. There was nothing a Hollywood director could conjure up that was worse than what I had to endure in my own home.

I loved my parents but I hated who they had become.

I hated my mother for getting drunk every day and hated my father for how he dealt with her. I know it must have been a sickening feeling to work all day and then come home to a drunken wife.

I withdrew, finding solace in my baseball cards. I'd play this game where I would dump all my cards out on the floor of my room and then randomly choose 25 without looking and that would be my "team." Of course, I would have to make trades with other imaginary teams to give my roster the balance it needed. I could escape there for hours at a time. Another game I'd play involved me putting on my New York Mets plastic replica batting helmet and imitating every Mets batter when they came to the plate as I listened to the games on the radio.

I really believed that if I got the stance down right and guessed correctly at what the pitcher was throwing then I could help the poor Mets get base hits. I can still hear play-by-play announcer Bob Murphy exclaim, "My oh my, those bases on balls," when I helped a Mets player draw a walk. I loved it. Before the age of cable television or satellite packages that allowed you to watch every baseball game, it was a magical time. It makes me sad to know for the majority of viewers now it is not the norm.

My dad moved out temporarily a couple of times. The last time I went out to the living room during one of their sessions I was still holding the baseball bat I was using to magically help the Mets. When my dad looked at the 32-inch long piece of lumber something must have clicked because he left the apartment and never beat her again.

My faith in God actually grew stronger during this time. I was old enough to go to church alone and I gladly chose the 7 p.m. Saturday evening mass. It was in English and there was usually no organist available so it lasted only 45 minutes or so. I just couldn't sit there any longer on Sunday pretending that I was part of this perfectly happy family.

I would sit in the back of the church and pray that things would change. If my dad was living with us then I prayed that my mother would stop drinking. If he had moved out temporarily then I prayed for him not to come home.

I had stopped being an altar boy and for the first time in my life I could listen to the sermons and try to understand the message of the gospel. I loved the parables, the stories of the miracles, and I especially loved the power of the crucifixion and resurrection narratives.

I loved being there. The scent of the candles burning and the incense filled me with peace. No one was drunk here and no one was being violent and I was safe. I still could not understand why Jesus had to die. Wouldn't it have been better for Him to just prove everyone wrong back then? Why not just show that He was the son of God? Why let them do all those despicable things to you?

It's a wonder to me now that I did not get more involved at St. Michaels parish, considering how I loved being there. I guess the options at that time were limited. There were no church youth groups or missions to help nurture my faith. There was no youth pastor to talk with and bounce ideas off. But as a young man I was also very lazy. I thought opportunities and success just sort of plopped down from nowhere onto your lap.

No, my faith was like the seed that got sprinkled among the rocks. It sprouted up, grew for a while, and then started to wither.

Of course, it didn't help that the parish priests stationed at St. Michael's were for the most part an uninspired lot. In fact, scandal even came to our parish when one of our pastors, Father Vincent Gorman, fell in love with the nun attached to our parish. They quit their respective holy orders and got married. That upset my mother deeply.

Despite all this, I gave great thought during this time to one day becoming a priest. But I never knew who to speak to about it or pursue it. I also worried that my stuttering, which got worse after every one of my parents' fights, would make me the world's worst priest. I mean, some sermons seemed too long even with an interesting and eloquent speaker.

Knowing it would never come true, I don't think I ever told anyone about my secret desire to become a priest. If I had known then what I know now then my life would probably have taken a different path.

But as thoughts of pursuing life as a priest faded slowly away, two names would define the path I was to take, even if my journey home seemed to take on so many unnecessary detours.

THREE

I MADE MY first real totally independent choice after graduating from the eighth grade. Having been a well-above average student, and having scored well on high school entrance exams, I pretty much had my choice of high schools to attend. There was the local Harry S. Truman High School, which was busing in students from some less than savory neighborhoods, the Bronx High School of Science, which was an elite school that lacked competitive sports teams, and finally my pick of any Catholic high school in the city.

I chose to attend Cardinal Spellman High School in the Bronx where I would be able to further my baseball career, play football for the first time, enjoy the coed environment, and hopefully thrive in the Jesuit-inspired discipline.

My decision bewildered many of my friends who would have given their right arm to be accepted into the Bronx High School of Science. But it thrilled my mother, who was proud that I'd be going to a Catholic school, where you were allowed to talk about Jesus and celebrate Christmas without the ACLU filing a lawsuit.

The school was predominantly Irish and Italian when I first enrolled and almost from day one I began experiencing something I never had before: racism. It was normally very subtle and in the form of joking but it was there. I felt it and now knew that people were capable of judging me without even bothering to get to know me.

Sports was an equalizer though and having made the freshman football team as a defensive tackle, I was no longer looked at as only a Puerto Rican by some, but as a jock. While they didn't accept me fully, I knew they tolerated me.

At no time in my life was racism so evident as when the school held baseball tryouts that spring. I was very excited to go out for the team and was confident that I would make it. The thought of walking around Co-op City with my red Spellman baseball windbreaker was just about all I could think of.

Since there were still several small mountains of snow out on the athletic fields, tryouts were held indoors. I knew the competition well from playing in all-star tournaments and sandlot teams. There were also many football players trying out. The competition would be very stiff.

But something peculiar happened after the very first day of the week-long tryout. Every black and Hispanic kid was cut from the squad after only one day of tryouts. All were gone but me.

It was blatant and what surprised me was how everyone knew it was going to happen since the team had been lily white from its inception. Before the tryouts began, some of my friends expressed concern that I wouldn't make it because no Latinos or blacks ever made it. I was stunned at the great ballplayers that never got the chance to play. It soured me.

Wasn't this supposed to be a Catholic school? Where were the Catholic principles? How could they, how could God allow such people the power to do what they were doing?

I wasn't cut the first day and as the week went on I know I impressed the coaches with my hustle, enthusiasm, and skills. Slowly but surely players were getting the bad news as the team was whittled down to about two dozen players. I knew I was better than at least half the players remaining and so I was confident that I would make the team.

Finally, when the moment of truth arrived, I was summoned into the coach's office where I made the team, but not really. He told me I was a very good player and that he wanted me on the team. The problem, he said, was that I was the 20th player and there were only 19 uniforms. I would be part of the team, practice and participate in every way imaginable, except for playing in the games. He told me to take the weekend to consider the offer because he knew I couldn't have been happy with the news.

My eyes welled with tears and I told him I would think about it, even though I knew at that instant that I would never play organized baseball again. I was stunned. It was as if someone kicked me in the gut. No uniform? I could see it now, "Gee dad I made the school baseball team but I will never play a game because they are one uniform short! Isn't that just the rottenest luck?"

It's funny but it was while attending Catholic high school that I first started drifting away from God. No, I have no horror stories of ruler-wielding Nazi nuns smacking wrists and thank God I have no stories to tell of how a pedophile disguised as a man of God took my innocence from me. It just didn't seem like a place that put God or Catholic principles first. I don't want it to sound like I'm bashing my old school or that I hold onto the bitterness of not making the baseball team. Neither is true.

I'm sure a lot of it had to do with me and where specifically I was on my journey at that particular point in my life. I went to school with the baggage my parents had saddled me with, without the lifetime friendships most of my new classmates enjoyed as they had attended Catholic elementary schools together, and with my insecurities growing as my stuttering problem increased.

Now, for the first time in my life, my classmates were laughing at my speech impediment. I became one of those students who kept his head down, tried not to make eye contact with anyone, and who got to school the very second it started and left as the tones from the final bells were still echoing through the halls.

Looking back, I can see how it just wasn't the right place for me at that time.

Back to the two names I mentioned earlier that would help shape some of my later decisions in life.

With my shot at a career as a professional baseball player dashed in high school, I wondered how else I could stay involved in the game that meant so much to me. Then one day while watching the Mets play baseball on television with my dad, the answer came to me. I was rattling off statistics, hometowns, and other trivial facts about my favorite players as they came to bat.

It caught my dad's attention. But when I started making dead-on predictions like "he'd better not throw him a fastball here or we could see a long ball," my dad said I would probably make a great sportscaster.

"My oh my, those bases on balls," I'd practice the signature Bob Murphy call. I'd go through the yearbooks and the rosters practicing how I would say everyone's name and then I hit the Pittsburgh Pirates and their star second baseman Rennie Stennett. I tried over and over again but just kept getting hung up on the ST sound of his last name. "Now coming to bat, second baseman Rennie St-st-st-stennett."

The slick fielding native of Panama will never know that he was the reason I could not pursue a career in the broadcast booth. Luckily, the second name was able to inspire me a few years earlier and has continued to do so for years.

That name was Ernest Hemingway and the second I finished reading *The Old Man and the Sea* I sort of knew that I would someday be a writer. I loved the simplicity of the story and the humility by which the "old man," Santiago, lived. I loved the religious imagery and was surprised to learn years later that Hemingway was not a believer.

To me it was obvious that the old man represented all that was good and had many Christlike qualities or moments. When the fishing line rips through his hands cutting deep into his palms, I couldn't help but think of the wounds Jesus suffered, the stigmata. Then, of course, when the old man returns to his sleepy fishing village, seemingly defeated but truly triumphant, he falls carrying his mast several times before arriving home.

Unlike Jesus, however, he did not have a Simon nearby to help him carry his "cross."

The book was lovely and soon I was devouring everything Hemingway wrote from the love story *The Sun Also Rises*, to the rum-running adventure *To Have and Have Not*.

I started writing. I continued reading. And if Hemingway did not see God, I saw God in the things he wrote. I kept journals. I wrote short stories and I even made a few feeble attempts at trying to write a novel. But writing is funny. Everyone thinks they can do it and it's actually a lot tougher than it looks. I was getting frustrated at how awful I was at it.

But then one Christmas my parents bought me a book that basically contained every article Hemingway wrote as a reporter for the *Kansas City Star* newspaper. Hmm, these pieces were a lot shorter than I had been attempting and yet still packed a wallop. Newspaper reporter started sounding like a good option until I could write that best-seller.

My dad liked to remind me that I was a Hemingway fan even before I read anything he wrote. Years earlier, before the age of multiplexes, when they still showed double-features in the local movie theater, you didn't need a credit card to buy popcorn and candy, and everything was prefaced by a Bugs Bunny cartoon, we went to see a movie called *Islands in the Stream*, starring George C. Scott.

To this day I lose it whenever I hear David ask his father in the movie if he's too old to kiss his father goodnight.

Hemingway had finished this novel shortly before taking his life but it was edited after his suicide. What my dad remembers a lot more clearly than I can is that it was the first time he ever saw me cry watching a movie.

I guess there's just something about his stories that affected me greatly.

By the time I was a high school senior at Cardinal Spellman High School, I had started playing keyboards in a rock band started by some friends, was dating girls, and was starting to experiment with drugs and alcohol.

God was an afterthought, though I still attended mass regularly on Saturday evenings. I was only going through the motions. I sat there, looking as interested as I could but the truth was I could not stop thinking about what plans my friends and I had in store. More often than not, it involved beer, marijuana, and girls.

I did sometimes feel badly that I couldn't even give God my full attention for one hour a week. But despite my turning my back on Him, He never turned His back on me. Despite my laziness and penchant for partying, God pushed me to overcome my stuttering to join the high school newspaper named *The Pilot*.

My first few pieces were about high school rock bands and either the editor was uninspired or I was a better writer than I thought. The pieces were published in the school paper exactly as I had written them, word for word.

It was an absolute thrill to see my name in print—written by John A. Torres. Wow. I was hooked. I knew from then on that this was what I wanted to do. But I was young and arrogant and never considered that I would need God's help to achieve my goals.

My parents, despite their flaws, were always supportive of my dreams. In fact, I think my dad may have been more excited about seeing my bylines. He instantly started a file—yes, he had a home filing cabinet system where he kept our report cards, book reports, essays, finger paintings, and other treasures created at school—and where he also kept my bylines. To this day, he keeps my more important stories and special investigative reports. He also has the jacket of every book that I have written, framed and hanging on his wall. He has more of my clips than I do.

My dad loved to come home from work with what he called "cositas," which is Spanish for "a little something." Those little somethings could be comic books or chocolate covered jelly rings, banana-flavored popcorn or plastic models. But as I got older and more interested in writing, those "cositas" became books. He'd bring me anything and everything about Hemingway from an obscure collection of poems to numerous biographies.

Looking back now, I'm sure he was trying to be the father he wished he'd had. There was no one to fuel his dreams as a kid. People were born in the ghettos of Washington Heights and lived their whole lives there. A Puerto Rican kid from the slums growing up in the 40s and 50s? I'm sure there wasn't a whole lot of hope.

But my dad is a history buff who probably knows more about World War II than most history teachers. I'll bet if he was given the kind of encouragement he gave me then he would have spent his formidable years in a tweed jacket giving lectures instead of sweating over repairs at a shaver shop.

Playing music was fun.

Like the rush I got from seeing my name in print, I loved the cheering—when they cheered us—of the crowd. I knew I was one of those personalities—and still am—that loves to be the center of attention. I need to tell the jokes at parties or show up with the best-looking girl or laugh the loudest. It's one of those weird quirks that I just cannot squash. It's all I can do to keep it under control and many times that takes a total and conscious effort not to be loud or an attention-hog. You have no idea how many times I have wanted to be low-key at a party or function and wound up stealing the limelight or making a fool of myself trying.

So being on stage, though nerve-wracking, was also intoxicating. And my dad, as he had done with my writing, was as supportive and encouraging as a father could be. He bought me synthesizers and music stands, microphones, drum machines, and even a small sound-system. That wasn't all. Before the four of us in the band had our driver's licenses, my dad would drive us from the Bronx to New Rochelle and our rehearsal studio. He also showed up at every gig we had at a dive of a bar in Yonkers called the Rising Sun.

When I told him I found a used piano that I wanted to get that would help me strengthen my fingers and technique, he insisted on buying a new one. He also paid for my piano lessons with Victor Talarico.

Mr. Talarico was the music teacher at Cardinal Spellman who also gave lessons at his beautiful home in Yonkers. He was also the father of Aerosmith front man Steven Talarico, whom the world knows as Steve Tyler.

He was a stern but funny little man and I enjoyed our chats at the keyboard as much as I did our lessons. He was full of life stories and experiences that I found fascinating and he was probably the closest thing I had to a "Tuesdays with Morrie" mentor.

Even to this day, I feel funny not calling him Mr. Talarico. Anyhow, he always split the lessons into two parts: the first half-hour he spent teaching me to read music and to learn technique. The second half-hour was spent helping me figure out parts of songs that I needed to learn for my rock band, Destiny.

His basement was homage to his famous son. The walls were plastered with gold records, photos, and other memorabilia. With all that stuff he probably could have served as the president of the Aerosmith fan club. But I will always remember feeling amazed that his world inside of a million-dollar home in the suburbs and my small apartment in the Bronx were both plagued by the same affliction.

It was during one of our lessons that his wife called down to the basement for him to take a phone call. He apologized profusely before running up the stairs to take it. He must have been gone for at least 15 minutes and I was worried that I would get hung up in traffic on the Saw Mill River Parkway on my way home.

I looked around, afraid of standing up and breaking something, and admired the gold records and other things. Then

I tinkered on the piano a little more. When he finally came downstairs, he apologized again but this time he looked different than I had ever seen him. He actually had a grin on his face from ear to ear, which surprised me because he wasn't what you'd call a joyous-looking man.

He sat down next to me on the keyboard and for a moment it seemed as if he couldn't speak. After a moment he turned to me and smiled once again.

"That was Steve on the phone," he said. "They're back in the studio working."

"That's cool," I replied, wondering privately what all the fuss was about.

"That was the first time in 10 years that I've spoken to my son and he was sober," he explained. There were tears in his eyes.

"That's great," I smiled back. "I had no idea."

And that was true. I had no idea that someone like Mr. Talarico, a man who seemingly had everything from a new Cadillac, to a string of cottages in New England, to a home in Florida and a famous son, could suffer with an alcoholic family member the same way I had.

From that day on I looked at Mr. Talarico a bit differently. He was no longer the strict, little piano teacher with the bulletproof life, but instead a vulnerable, old friend.

I got accepted into Fordham University, which was my second choice after Columbia University. I wanted to get into the best journalism program I could. For a while I considered NYU, but the idea of hanging out down in the East Village didn't entice me. There was something about the gothic, majestic buildings on Fordham's campus and, though I'm not sure why, I was drawn to the idea of going to a Catholic college.

Fordham was and is still run by Jesuits and I thought that was kind of cool.

The band split up shortly after we all started college. I wasn't as broken up about it as the other three fellas were. I knew there was no way we would ever make it as successful, famous rock stars. We simply were not good enough and definitely not dedicated enough to ever go very far. I took it for what it was: An awesome experience that let me meet a lot of interesting people and a lot of pretty girls.

I never worked hard enough learning to play the piano or keyboards to become very good. I still have the piano my father bought me and one of these days, I keep promising myself, I'll go back for piano lessons.

I recently looked up Mr. Talarico. He is in his 90s and living in New England. I called a phone number associated with his address a couple of times recently, but I never heard back. I wonder if he'd remember me. It has, after all, been about 25 years. And I'm sure that he made a much bigger impression on me than I did on him.

I was done with the keyboard when I started college. No, I knew my future would involve the written word, but I never thought it would involve God.

When my mom and dad finally stopped hurting each other, I noticed they started going to church together more often than they had in the past. Funny, but I always assumed the break in their volatility to simply be advancing age and having nothing at all to do with spirituality.

Fordham University was a good school and I made a few real close friends. But, if I could do it over, I likely would have opted to go away to school. As a "muter," short on campus for commuter, you were often left out of fun things going on campus or simply learned of them too late.

So, very much like my experience in high school, I showed up for classes then left immediately after. I never went to football games or basketball games, campus dances or on class trips. If I stayed it was normally only to play racquetball with my friend, Artie.

That's not to say I didn't enjoy my classes. The film classes I took as part of my communications degree requirements were fascinating and I still amaze my family when I press the pause button and point out a prop, or shadow, or other technique being used in a scene. I took a television production class as well as a film editing course and loved them both. But I excelled at writing, and the journalism classes were my favorite.

During my first two years at Fordham, I spent most of my free time working on one novel or another, feeling that every time I put my pen to paper I was at the very least honing my craft. At best? Maybe I was sitting on a best-seller. Of course, that hasn't happened yet. But I also landed a very cool job that didn't pay much but it gave me the credibility I was looking for.

I started working as a "stringer" or freelance writer for the *Enterprise* newspaper based in Hastings, NY. The small weekly tabloid covered the four adjoining Hudson Valley communities of Dobbs Ferry, Ardsley, Irvington, and of course Hastings.

My assignments ranged from covering the slow goings-on at town council meetings, to profiles of award-winning school teachers, to my weekly "Police Beat" feature, which consisted of me driving to the four police stations in our coverage area and looking at the police blotters.

This was where anyone can go and look at the calls taken by the dispatcher. Most of the calls involved domestic violence and alcohol, something I was all too familiar with, and the remainder were bar fights, traffic stops or shoplifting cases.

One of my favorite assignments ever in my career was to do a story about a local judge who had angered some of his neighbors in an upscale neighborhood by not trimming his grass often enough, allowing it to reach jungle-like proportions. They took him to court and he was ordered to mow his grass, to keep it trim.

He was an old rickety man who looked as if his face had gotten stuck in a permanent scowl after eating a bowl of lemons.

So what did he do? He bought a pair of bleating goats and let them loose in his yard! Sure they kept the grass trim but the smell was awful and it was actually quite shocking in his exclusive housing development. That's one clip I wish I had saved.

This was still in the pre-computerized era and my editors requested that I type—yes, on a typewriter—my stories in column form on yellow paper. Then I would cut my stories into the columns and drive to Dobbs Ferry to submit them. I'm not sure how they went from my yellow typed pages to the stories in the newspaper but there, once again, was my name in print. And, at $15 an article, I was a professional writer!

There was no need for me to volunteer at Fordham's prestigious school newspaper or write copy for our very popular radio station, WFUV. It never occurred to me that more people probably read the school paper than the *Enterprise*. Nope, in my head I was definitely too good to write for free!

I cruised through classes, never applying myself more than was needed to score a B in a class. It's scary how well I did in school without exerting any real effort. If I had applied myself I probably could have been a brain surgeon, though knowing how incredibly squeamish I am at the site of blood, that probably wouldn't have been a good idea.

The closest thing I had to a religious experience during my college years was listening to the U2 album, "The Joshua Tree." I remember being in my burgundy Dodge Aspen driving home one afternoon from class and hearing "With or Without You," for the first time. I'm not exactly sure what Bono had in mind when writing those lyrics but the song was personal for me, as was much of the album. I felt the song was about my relationship with God. "With or without you, I can't live, . . ." the lyrics went.

I was frustrated that God was not an active part of my life. I knew that was my decision but I couldn't figure out how to include Him. Other songs on the album hit religious nerves for me as well. The song "I Still Haven't Found What I'm Looking For" expressed almost to a tee what I was feeling about God and religion. And I knew that the song "Where the Streets Have No Name," was about heaven, or at least my version of it.

Music was often a nice escape for me and to this day I sometimes drive my wife nuts by listening to music all day long. I'd like to give a big hug to the guy or gal that first dreamt up the iPod. I also found a lot of meaning and time for reflection by watching movies. I even studied them during my years at Fordham.

I remember my buddy Artie coming over so we could cram together for the final exam of one of our film courses. The topic was the American Western and we had analyzed dozens of movies and learned twice as many technical terms that we would now be tested on.

Of course Artie brought over some beer and chips and soon our study session was instead focused on whether the New York Knicks would win an NBA world championship any time in the next 100 years. Sadly, the consensus was a big fat no.

It wasn't until midnight, when the beer ran out, that we both sort of realized that we were going to be in big trouble on this test. That's when I remembered that our professor often spoke of a film we did not see as a class but that contained many elements important to the Western—a stranger with a dangerous past and a heart of gold, an innocent child drawn to the dangerous stranger, a greedy land baron, and a hired assassin—Shane!

I tore open my dad's video cabinet and found the videotape. There it was, the holy grail of Western films, Alan Ladd as Shane.

I convinced Artie that all we needed to do was watch *Shane*, maybe take a few notes and we'd be fine. So that's exactly what we did. We watched, or I should say I watched, while Artie snored. He slept over and we struggled to make it to class the following morning. My entire essay dealt with Shane and how it related to the entire genre. I scored an A. Artie muddled through with a low C.

By junior year I had completed my share of required classes and was now taking a slew of journalism and writing classes. No longer would I have to pretend to be awake during philosophy classes or to get my head around medieval history. Now I could concentrate on learning to become a good newspaper writer.

The class that changed things for me was called "Basic Journalistic Techniques" and it was taught by a writer who worked as a fact checker for the *New York Times*. I liked having a professor who actually worked in the field he was teaching and he was a pretty nice guy. Then one day he asked if there was anyone in the class interested in becoming a sports writer. My hand shot up as quickly if not quicker than the 20 other guys and two girls who also answered yes.

Then he proceeded to write down the phone number for the editor at United Press International, still a formidable wire service that competed with the Associated Press. He said they were looking for interns to help work during the baseball season.

I could hardly contain myself. Sports? Baseball?

Being Oscar Madison, or Mike Lupica, Red Smith, or any other of my favorite fictional or factual sports writers, was a very low second to being the next Ernest Hemingway, but it was second nonetheless. I called immediately after school (there were no such things as cell phones yet) and was instructed where to send my letter of interest and resume.

I went out and bought a book of Red Smith columns. I'm pretty sure he's the guy who wrote, "Writing is easy, just open a vein and bleed on the page." I know that's awfully corny, but I always loved that saying. Maybe because I know how true it is.

But I was also insecure about my speech and my talent. I was never quite sure if the things I wrote were any good or if they should be used to line the bottom of the parakeet cage.

But a Hemingway quote about writing, written to his wife Mary, gave me comfort.

"Nobody really knows or understands and nobody has ever said the secret. The secret is that it is poetry written into prose and it is the hardest of all things to do," he wrote.

It was hard for him? He was insecure? Maybe I did have a chance after all.

I mailed out my resume as I was told but also realized there was probably no way I was going to land that internship. At least 22 other students in my class were making that same phone call. And who knows in how many classes my professor made the same announcement.

But after a few days I couldn't get it out of my mind and I decided to call. No decision yet. Please call back. And so I did, daily for about two weeks. Finally, they asked me when I could start!

To make it better, it was an actual paying job, not just an internship for credit. I would be paid $9.34 an hour and work nights for 35 hours a week. That's a great paycheck for a 19-year-old college student. They would be paying me to write about Major League Baseball. Shoot, I would have done that job for free. I got to go to ball games and meet famous athletes. It was a thrill to sit in the visiting manager's office at Yankee Stadium and listen to Orioles' manager Earl Weaver talk about the game.

The first day I met Kevin Kenny, my desk editor, he said the only reason he gave me the job was so that I would quit calling every day asking about it.

I've told that story to my kids many times.

The job wasn't so much writing as it was compiling statistics for the small print in the sports pages called agate and taking dictation over the phone. Still, it was an awesome job with a great bunch of guys and I was lucky to have it. Did I thank God? Of course not. This was something I did on my own without anyone's help. That's what I thought anyhow.

Balancing a full-time class load with a full-time job was actually a lot easier than I expected. It wasn't like I was applying myself or immersing myself in my studies. No, I did the least I could do to get by. Plus, did I really need to do well in school? I already had a dream writing job and my life was certain to only get better. I was on top of the world.

I started spending money on silly things like a Sinatra-style fedora, computer games, trips on spring break to Florida and an earring for my newly pierced ear. I remember my grandmother "Mamita's" reaction when she saw me wearing an earring for the first time.

She calmly sat down, started eating her dinner, and in Spanish asked me what I was protesting against.

"Huh?" I didn't understand.

"Well, the only men who would wear earrings are men who are protesting something, you know, rebelling against society."

I smiled and couldn't have felt sillier. She was right. What did I have to rebel against? I only kept that earring in for the next 20 years. I took it out when I turned 40.

The job was wonderful and the crew of misfits, alcoholics, and coke-heads made for some interesting times. It was almost as if they were my night-school teachers. We'd work from 7 p.m. until 2:30 in the morning or sometimes later when there was late-night West Coast baseball. Inevitably, on the nights you wanted to get out at a decent hour, the Seattle Mariners and Oakland Athletics or any other pair of worthless last-place teams would hook up in a meaningless 18-inning ballgame.

Even though I was a lifelong Mets fan, I will always remember the evening that our senior baseball writer, Mike Tully, took me with him to cover a Yankee game. The hairs on my neck and arms stood straight up as we walked right past home plate, the same spot where decades earlier players like Babe Ruth and Joe DiMaggio had stood ready to stare down the pitcher. The grass was incredibly green and bounced like a cushion beneath my sneakers.

The air smelled of popcorn and beer and even the fluttering of the summer moths drawn to the stadium's lights seemed to happen majestically and in slow motion. Walking out onto that field almost felt holy.

I met and made a lifelong friend working for the sports department at UPI, Bill Wolle. Bill has since moved to Washington, D.C. and I wound up farther south in Florida. And it's funny, he's one of those friends that you can go six months without communicating with and then pick up as if you spoke to him yesterday.

Every year, Bill invites me to go to Spain and retrace Hemingway's steps by running with the bulls with him in Pamplona. I've never been able to go, usually due to financial reasons. But I told him to never stop asking. One of these summers I'll surprise him and do it.

After work we'd go swill beers and play arcade hockey and foosball at a bar across from the Daily News building in midtown Manhattan where the UPI offices were located. That's where I learned first-hand that cocaine was more prevalent than God in a newsroom. In fact, I was surprised that just about everyone I met was an atheist.

Anyhow, it's ridiculous and embarrassing to think about how many nights, or should I say mornings, that I drove home to the Bronx drunk and sleepy only to have to wake up in a few hours for class. Luckily, I never got arrested or had an accident and never missed a class—until the last final exam of my collegiate career, that is.

It's funny. I know many people who have recurring nightmares about missing exams in school or finding themselves out in public wearing their pajamas.

Well, I did both.

After a late night at UPI, where I had instituted the office wave—everyone would stand one at a time from their desks and wave their arms in the air as if they were at a sporting event—followed by several beers at Mumbles, I must have slept through my alarm clock's annoying tweet, tweet. Normally that wouldn't have been a problem, except when I looked at the time I realized that I was already one hour into my two-hour political science final exam. I seriously leapt from my bed and I think I stayed airborne for several seconds, flittering like a hummingbird desperately searching for clean clothes on my carpeted floor.

I darted around looking, searching but there was nothing. I

couldn't tell what was clean from what should have been put in the hamper days ago.

When I finally came crashing down, I knew it would take me 15 minutes to drive to school, five additional minutes to run to class, and then 40 minutes to take the test. There was not a second to spare to look for clothes. I threw on my army surplus jacket and stole a glance in the mirror.

Crud still in eyes: check.

Bad breath film and saliva smeared on lips: check.

A case of pillow hair that would make the Heat Miser jealous: check.

A three-day-old case of 5 o'clock shadow: check.

Left unchecked were underwear, proper shirt, or pants.

Instead, I ran out of the house looking like some lunatic attempting to escape the insane asylum he knows he's in by mistake. I didn't care. There was no time to.

I burst into the classroom feeling like Santa Claus after discovering he'd skipped a house the night before and was trying to get it right on December 26. I whisked past Artie who looked up from his papers and gave me the "what the fudge?" look.

I heaved a sigh of relief, didn't care that I was wearing very thin blue and white striped pajamas, and took the test. For the sake of the others in the class, I left my army coat on the entire time.

I got a B on the test and graduated in May 1987.

One of my greatest memories is that my grandmother, "Mamita," was there at the Rose Hill campus to see me earn my diploma, earring and all.

FOUR

A FEW MONTHS after graduation, the place I loved to work, the place where I thought I would move on up through the ranks and became a famous writer, the wire service known as United Press International began to go belly up.

My editor Kevin Kenny had already landed a job with Gannett and another coworker, Steve Rutkowski, jumped ship to work for ESPN. I wasn't so lucky. I kept showing up for work until I looked at the work schedule and noticed that my name was missing from the following week's rotation.

What a kick in the pants that was.

The executive editor, Fred McMane, called me into his office and apologized. It was about cutbacks and trimming expenses with hopes the company would be sold, blah, blah, blah.

I was so insulted that I felt like leaving right then and there but I stayed and worked my shift for the rest of the week. My dad advised me not to burn any bridges and so I was courteous and respectful. It wasn't hard to do; I liked everyone who worked there.

Welcome to the real world.

During this time, my older sister, Maryellen, asked me if I would be her daughter Ally's godfather. I was thrilled, of course, but also suddenly wracked with guilt. Isn't a child's godfather supposed to be someone who would be a spiritual role model? Someone who would lead the child through her faith and be there if her parents couldn't? Someone who was in harmony with his faith and in communion with the Catholic church?

I was none of those things and I became ashamed.

No, I had stopped going to church altogether. I experimented with drugs, drank too much, did things with women I didn't care about and really only worried for my well-being. Maybe I would be a perfect role model for someone looking to fall away from the church.

In fact, I can laugh now at this, but I even started studying the teachings of Lao Tzu and the Way of Life because, as I said back then, "It feels like Christianity without all the negativity." The books were filled with clever little sayings I could rattle off. Teachings that would allow me to spoon-feed myself whatever I wanted spiritually and at the same time do whatever I pleased.

And even though I loved the sayings and the ideals of humility and self-denial, I never practiced it. I still have a Lao Tzu book and found a passage I circled: "The wise man, therefore, while he is alive, will never make a show of being great; and that is how his greatness is achieved."

Maybe I circled it because it was the opposite of who I was. If I had spent my time reading the bible instead of ancient Chinese mystics then perhaps my life would have turned out differently. But I also believe that this is the path God has set for me and there must be reasons for all the bumps and potholes I caused myself to careen into during my long journey home.

I guess my one attribute during this time was that I knew I was a worthless sinner. I knew others, just like me, who lied to themselves about being good, practical Catholics. So, at least being able to recognize how far away from God I had fallen, I approached my sister with the news that I would have to decline her request that I be her daughter's godfather. I shouldn't have been surprised that everyone in my family jumped down my throat and insisted I was being ridiculous and, of course, I was more than qualified to serve in that capacity.

So I did.

And luckily, my old UPI editor, Kevin Kenny, hired me as a sports writer working for Gannett and their Westchester/Rockland newspapers. The pay was only $8 an hour and it was part-time work at 25 hours a week, but at least I'd be working and get to see my name in print again.

I was covering local college basketball and some high school sports. This was a far cry from chatting with Earl Weaver in his office, but it would do for now.

A few months after starting to work for Gannett, I experienced something I never had before: a broken heart. It didn't matter that I cheated on her, or treated her like a girl instead of a woman, or would often drop her off at her home so I could go out with my friends and meet other girls. I was still shocked when my girlfriend—Rosemarie—slid a letter under the door to my apartment one Sunday morning.

"Dear John (seriously)," is how the letter started. You can fill in the blanks for the rest. I was devastated. Of course, when I looked back, even just a few weeks later, it made perfect sense. I wasn't a good person. What made me think I was a good boyfriend? I was getting perfect training to be a bad husband as well.

Only a few weeks and a few one-night stands later, I met my first wife. A street-wise, gum-cracking bleached blonde with very high hair that must have 20 years later inspired the "bump-it" hair insert. But she was exactly what I thought I was looking for and very different from anyone I had ever dated. I used to go for the cerebral, plain-Jane types. Remember the Ivory girl? No makeup, jeans, and a football shirt? Those were the type I dated.

But my future wife was the exact opposite. She never went to college, worked as a waitress, spent her money at dance clubs on the weekends, loved to gossip, and had an opinion about everything. I know she wasn't very intelligent but at the time it seemed charming. I found her to be a breath of fresh air.

Of course, I knew I was on a total rebound but it didn't matter. I was having a good time and I would ride it out for as long as it lasted. Of course, it lasted a lot longer than it should have.

We moved in together and starting playing house. It was a tiny little apartment in Throgs Neck that was actually a converted garage. We had some laughs there and nothing ever really seemed serious until, of course, she became pregnant.

Not really ready to face life as parents, we drove to an abortion clinic in Yonkers. We sat silently for the entire ride there as if something had suddenly changed in the relationship. Even though we were both lapsed Catholics, we both recognized the sanctity of life. Once we saw the protestors outside the clinic, we decided to turn around and return to the Bronx.

Daniel John Torres was born nine months later on November 10, 1990 and I never thought I was capable of loving someone so much.

Watching my parents interact with my son also showed me how much love they were capable of as well. It warmed me to know that they once held me in their arms in the very same way. I felt newly committed to being a great father and a better person. I gave up on my dream of being the next Ernest Hemingway and I got a steady, reliable job as a hospital carpenter at Albert Einstein College of Medicine in the Bronx. I also gave up my dream of reeling in a marlin—like Santiago in *The Old Man and the Sea*—and cancelled a Hawaiian fishing trip that my father had planned to give me and instead asked him for the cash so I could put a down payment on a townhouse in Dutchess County.

It never dawned on me that this plan to become a great dad and better person should involve God. I was already living the dream without Him.

But that dream slowly began to deteriorate and plunge to nightmarish proportions. The things about my wife that I initially found charming lost their luster after not too long. Her negativity, gossiping, and sniping behind everyone's back became a drain. Then when she was forced to stop working because of a bad back and started staying home, our finances went from the treading water category to one of ruin.

She had no ambition. She refused to go back to school or find a job she could handle even as the bank foreclosed on our townhouse, forcing us into bankruptcy. We stayed in Dutchess

County, though I'm not sure why as I had a 65-mile one-way commute to my carpenter job in the Bronx every day.

I'd come home from work every day simply exhausted and then had to deal with her depression.

"I'm bored," she'd lament, as I cleared the ice from my eyebrows after trudging into the house.

"Well, I'm not supposed to be your entertainment. I'm supposed to be your husband," I thought, but never said it, knowing it would only make things worse.

Instead I drove to all the nearby colleges and brought home course catalogs. I sent away for information about interior decorating school. I scoured the want ads for jobs that seemed like fun. I encouraged joining women's groups to make friends.

Meanwhile, I continued to chase my dreams of becoming a writer. I sent book proposals to numerous publishers. I was trying to sell a book idea about the history of baseball in New York. No one nibbled though one publisher did call one day and asked if I would be interested in writing a biography for kids about baseball superstar Darryl Strawberry.

It was a dream come true. I was going to be a published author.

I spent the next few months spending my lunch hour writing. I researched; I interviewed teammates and former teammates and coaches. I poured my heart and soul into that book and finally I was a published author. Of course, I thought my future as a writer was set in stone. But something funny happened on the way to fame and fortune. No one was interested in a second book.

In fact, it took five years to get a publisher to agree to give me a contract for another book, followed by another and another. Those little books, where I made about $1,000 in advances and a small percentage of royalties, kept me going. They were my escape from the world I was living in and my hope for a future.

"Are you trying to say you're not happy with the person I am? Are you trying to change who I am?" my wife would scold me whenever I returned home with papers for college or groups I thought she might be interested in.

I shook my head internally and threw my hands in the air.

We found a small condominium to rent and she took herself off of birth control without my knowledge and became pregnant.

She later said she thought it would help save our marriage. I'll always be indebted for the gift of Jacqueline Nicole Torres, born on December 11, 1995, but by that time we had started growing seriously apart and it was only a matter of time.

Adding to my burgeoning malaise, my parents and my two sisters moved to Florida. I was alone and I felt alone.

We trudged on trying to make the situation work and every time we passed St. Mary, Mother of the Church in Fishkill, I found an old familiar comfort and mentioned that we should start going to services.

But my wife was not interested and so, as I had done so many years before to escape my parents, I started attending Saturday evening services, alone. I sat in the back, away from everyone and took in the aroma of incense, the slow melodies of the pipe organ and began to think about my life. Was this really it? Was I resigned to living with a woman I no longer loved, always under the strain of financial hardship?

The charm of working with my hands as a carpenter also quickly lost its appeal as I was often the subject of ridicule for being the only "college-educated maintenance man" there. It didn't help that I could only muster being a mediocre carpenter as well.

My self-esteem began to suffer and even the idea of sitting in God's house alone for an hour every Saturday night didn't seem to help. I allowed my wife to start treating me in ways I never thought possible.

She systematically broke me down. She alienated me from my family, from my friends and even from God when she started complaining about having to take care of the children while I went to mass. It wasn't worth the aggravation; it wasn't worth the arguing. So I stopped going to church.

Writing became my religion. My books, as little and insignificant as they were, became my salvation. I shared some of my feelings with my carpenter shop foreman, Paul Saltzman, who also became my friend. I told him that I wished I could write something more substantial, something that could really touch lives.

Then I started receiving the occasional letter from some inner-city kid who had read one of my books. They'd say things like "This was the best book I have ever read," or "Your book makes me want to become a writer too."

I shared these with Paul and he shook his head.

"Don't you see?" he asked. "What a legacy you are leaving behind. If they print 10,000 books and only 20 percent or 10 percent are affected by it then you will have left a positive impact on 1,000 children with every book. Now that's something."

For two years I slept on the couch as things between us worsened. My wife told me that no woman would ever be interested in me and that I was lucky she had taken pity on me. I started to believe it. Her family was not supportive either. Thriving on conflict and discord, they often picked fights with my wife and myself, alienating us from any family.

I became more broken than I already was.

It's very hard for me to admit this in writing, but I even thought of killing myself. I had stopped looking out for God but He must have been looking out for me. Despite my despair, I realized I wanted to stay alive.

But just as I started to hit rock bottom, I answered a help-wanted ad for the local newspaper, the only daily paper in all of Dutchess County: *The Poughkeepsie Journal*. They gave me a chance and I was soon writing for them as a freelance contributor. I wrote riveting articles about new programs at the local library, profiles of new teachers hired at the elementary school and even a story about a Boy Scout leader for the weekly "Neighbor" feature. None of the topics or subjects would put me in Pulitzer consideration, but I was having a blast.

My wife did not like it but this would be the first time I had the nerve to defy her.

I had forgotten the joy I received from writing. She resented the time it took away from her, but I was not going to give this up. I would even spend my lunch breaks from my carpentry job on the phone interviewing subjects for my stories. I remember one fun story was about a very famous diner in the Hudson Valley that was being lifted, apple pie and all, off the ground and moved to a new location.

My very first front page story happened when I was asked to fill in for the education reporter to cover a Wappingers Falls School Board meeting. When the board moved to oust one of its members I got thrown into a mild panic.

"Uh, this wasn't on the agenda," I thought.

Thankfully I rushed to the phone and called the night editor. I was known as a pretty reliable stringer after that.

One assignment led to another and I even worked alongside staffers on election night in the newsroom. Before long I was invited to interview for a staff writing position and I was offered the position of education reporter.

I wasn't worthless. Someone wanted to hire me. Someone asked for and cared to hear my opinions. Someone saw something that I had long missed. My commute went from 90 minutes to 15 minutes and I would be back doing something I loved.

I was a writer for an award-winning daily newspaper!

Of course, my wife was suffering from such extreme depression that she could not be truly happy for me. She complained about the hours, about the health benefits, about the person who answered the phone when she called to speak with me at the paper.

I received accolades, awards, notoriety, and was even sent on trips and conferences. Of course, any good feeling about being the only staffer chosen to attend a newspaper conference in Washington, D.C. evaporated under her complaints that she would be "stuck" with the children while I was gone.

My home life was miserable but I was not going to let it affect my career. I loved going to work and the people who actually respected me. They wanted to hear my ideas. They liked me.

One year after being hired, I was promoted to the Assistant City Editor position. This, while accompanied with a pretty significant pay increase, also meant that I would have to work later hours—sometimes until after 11 p.m. Needless to say that was not a very positive development in my home.

In addition to my daily duties, I was in charge of the Monday newspaper. Every local word that appeared in Monday's editions was assigned by me, read by me, and edited by me. Of course, if something major happened on a Sunday then it was my responsibility to get into the office, call in reporters, and redo the newspaper.

There is a certain rush you get from working at a newspaper, especially when something big is happening. Everyone is talking, yelling, making phone calls, rushing around the newsroom, spilling coffee. It's quite exciting, like the time when the town of Poughkeepsie's Police Department had arrested someone in connection with more than a half dozen missing prostitutes.

Being the first one in the newsroom that day, I was sent straight out to 99 Fulton Avenue—the home of Kendall Francois, an obese African-American man who had killed the women and positioned them throughout the home he shared with his parents. The rumor was that he continued to do terrible things to the women long after they were dead. When police opened the door, the stench of death was enough to make you gag. It crept out of the house like a fog that seemed to hang over this modest Poughkeepsie neighborhood near Vassar College for the next few weeks.

There were reporters there from the *New York Times*, the *New York Daily News* and television trucks were parked everywhere. I had never been part of such a big story and it was exciting and a relief that this monster was finally caught.

There is a rush of exhilaration when you find yourself contributing to something important and bigger than yourself. There is also a certain rush you feel when a member of the opposite sex starts showing interest in you.

And that was starting to happen a lot despite my marital status. Women in the office—or on assignment—beautiful women, started smiling at me, talking to me, asking me if I wanted to "hang out."

My present wife jokes that I have the "kavorka," the lure of the animal that "afflicted" the character of Kramer on the hit television series *Seinfeld*. Suddenly, women from all walks of life were being drawn to Kramer. And while that certainly was not happening to me, I was getting my fair share of advances.

And to be perfectly honest, I was enjoying it. Like the tigers at the Bronx Zoo's Wild Asia exhibit that are kept adjacent to the deer pen to keep their hunting instincts alive, mine were also being reawakened.

Now the idea of divorcing my wife was not one that I really entertained. I did not want to be separated from my children and I guess in a sense I was afraid of being alone. With no family around me to offer advice or support, I just figured that this would be my lot in life. There were certainly people in worse situations than I and if this was all there was, then so be it.

I started finding happiness in the little things of the day, like music or being the first to use the just cleaned rest rooms at the newspaper. I loved seeing the blue water sitting in the toilet bowl. I found happiness in catching the green lights along Route 9 on my way to work just right. I could sometimes make it from Fishkill to the newspaper in less than 10 minutes if I timed the traffic lights just right.

But the advances continued and I found myself facing a dilemma. Starved for the affections of another woman, I began a series of affairs. I was searching for something, anything, and unable to find it at home, I thought I could find it in the arms of someone else. It was exciting and scary all at the same time. I knew it was wrong but I forced myself not to care. The less I thought about it, the easier it became. I became very good at lying. Of course, in some strange, twisted way, I thought it was noble never to lie to the woman I was having the affair with. I never said I was leaving my wife; I never lied about my situation. In a way, the affairs were the only times I could find myself being truly honest with an intimate partner.

Still, I knew I wasn't some soulless monster who couldn't differentiate right from wrong. I knew I could not carry on this double and sometimes triple life indefinitely.

Like getting on a rollercoaster that you know is going to make you sick, I found it impossible to get off the ride. Every night I would stare at my reflection in the mirror and promise myself that I would stop doing what I was doing.

I knew it was wrong. No matter how badly I felt my wife was treating me, I knew that cheating on her was not the answer. And once again, during a period in my life when I should have been leaning on God for support, I didn't.

The next two years my life became a total lie. Looking to fill the emptiness in my life, I was sneaking around with several different women. I became an expert at juggling a demanding career, being a devoted father and Little League coach, husband, and cheater.

Finally, disgusted with my actions or ready to move on in a different direction, I allowed myself to get caught and I was exposed. I was asked, in no uncertain terms, to leave my home. Initially, there was relief and euphoria. But then I realized I was as confused as ever.

After a brief period of separation and bitterness where I was as lost as I had ever been, my wife asked me to return. Apologizing for the way she had treated me over the years, she pleaded with me to return. She promised things would get better, that we could have a fresh start.

I felt sorry for her. I was also worried that somehow she would be able to take my children away from me. If my parents were able to remain together there was no reason we couldn't either. I agreed and came home.

We decided to pack our things, leave the gray, snowy Hudson Valley behind, and move to Florida. Of course I was thrilled. We would finally be close to my family and away from hers.

And while I know this is not true, it certainly felt as if it snowed six inches every single day between October and April that last year we spent in New York.

In another wonderful twist of fate, or as my Christian friends like to say "a God thing," the editor who had first hired me in Poughkeepsie, was now the Executive Editor at *Florida Today*, a large daily paper serving Florida's Space Coast. We would be living close to world famous Cocoa Beach, the Kennedy Space Center and were only an hour away from Orlando and all the theme parks. There also seemed to be no shortage of bad news. It seemed as if Florida was a magnet for pedophiles, murderers and other riff-raff whose stories and mug shots belonged plastered on the front pages.

There was also good news to cover, like the shuttle program, space exploration and nearby Patrick Air Force Base.

I'll always remember the first time I heard the sonic boom of a shuttle making its way back to the Kennedy Space Center. It was about two in the morning and it nearly knocked me from my bed. I seriously thought a tractor-trailer had slammed into my garage. I leapt up, my heart trying to rip its way out of my chest, and ran to the garage.

Nothing.

I've learned since to always know when the shuttles are due back.

One of the things my wife and I had decided upon moving to Florida was that we would start going to church together. We attended Ascension Catholic Church in Melbourne and even met with Father Eamon Tobin to discuss some of the issues that were tearing our marriage apart. That was when I learned that my wife had cheated on me too!

She apologized through the tears and I forgave her. How could I not have? We attended mass, enrolled the kids in local sports leagues and life seemed to be good. It was nice to have God back in my life.

My son was a dominating left-handed pitcher and Jackie became this beautiful, athletic soccer player.

Strange, but one of the first things I noticed about working at *Florida Today* newspaper was how absent God seemed to be from the newsroom. It wasn't just that people kept their religious beliefs to themselves. There just seemed to be a lot of people who were positive that He did not exist and were only too happy to tell you how silly it is to believe in God. They were also pro-abortion, or as they liked to say: "pro-choice." I kept my beliefs to myself, mainly because I was no longer sure what I believed.

I was assigned a wonderful story during my first year to track a family of undocumented orange pickers for about a year and then fly to Mexico to see how their hard labor had benefited those left behind.

This was before anti-Mexican fervor landed over our country. I can't imagine the newspaper agreeing to do something like that in the present political climate.

This family was so gracious, hardworking, and generous. Every time my photographer and I visited, we would be forced to sit and eat dinner or lunch. They would prepare an elaborate meal every time we showed up. Whether it was carne frita or tortilla soup or enchiladas, we always felt guilty sitting down and eating what was likely the only food they had for the night. But they insisted and it actually would have insulted them had we refused.

Their yard was littered with broken bicycles they would fix, old truck engines they would try and rejuvenate, and other assorted items that I would consider trash were scattered about. Their furniture was also thrift store quality at best. The kitchen table was an old poker table with a piece of wood fitted atop covered by a plastic tablecloth. The utensils were a hodgepodge of several different sets and the television set had a wire hanger for an antennae.

The nicest thing in the small home was probably the beautifully framed picture they had hanging inside the house above the front door. It was the Sacred Heart of Jesus. You could feel the love in the home and knew that Jesus lived there, as He often does with the poor and destitute.

I was moved by this family's generosity and closeness. They had the type of love I wished my family had. The truth was that my wife and I had once again started drifting apart and she began accusing me of "dragging" her to Florida, away from her family and friends. I guess she had forgotten that the move was her idea.

The depression had once again set in.

I was also inspired by how hard the family worked. The husband toiled all day breaking his back picking oranges during the season and digging trenches for water sprinkler systems in the off-season. His wife cleaned people's houses, did their laundry, watched children, anything to make ends meet.

They worked six days a week and on the seventh day they honored God by going to Our Lady of Guadalupe Catholic Church in Fellsmere. They made it special too by making a big breakfast before going and then dressing up in their absolute best clothes.

It made me embarrassed that they had time to go to church but I didn't. Even though I needed His help and guidance the most, I still could not bring myself to ask. Part of it though had to do with the sin I was carrying.

After what I had done, how could I possibly be worthy of God's love?

The trip to a small area of Central Mexico called Zacatlan de las Manzanas was incredible and beautiful. The hills were literally blanketed with purple and yellow flowers and almost anywhere you looked could have turned into a postcard. The generosity of the people in the states sending their money back to mothers, brothers, cousins, and sisters was not exclusive to them. The people we visited, total strangers really, welcomed us as if we were the family members sending back the money we earned picking fruit.

The story was published in a 52-page special section—with no ads—dubbed "El Sueno" or "the dream." It went on to win several journalism awards, my first. Several local teachers wrote me letters saying they would be using it in the classrooms and likened it to the *Grapes of Wrath* and *Uncle Tom's Cabin*.

I was humbled by their words. It was at that moment that I realized I could do this job and be really good at it.

An offshoot of the project was that I met a local attorney, Steve, who happened to represent the Mexican family on a matter they were trying to resolve. I talked him into speaking with me though he had a serious distrust of the media and over the years we developed a good friendship. It's funny, I have a lawyer friend named Steve and a doctor friend named Steve.

Professionally my career was taking off. But at home things were terrible. My wife reverted to her old ways and I was finding escape in music and my new treadmill. She did not understand that the new business is not always a 9 to 5 gig and that there were many days where I had to stay until six or later. She flipped out when I had to cover the occasional night meeting at Palm Bay City Hall or in Malabar.

Again I tried to get her involved in hobbies or classes she was interested in. I finally got her to volunteer some time at the Wildlife Sanctuary on U.S. 1 in Melbourne where injured animals were nursed back to health.

She went twice and was discouraged that she spent her entire time doing laundry one day and preparing cereal for injured birds the second day. I guess she expected that she'd be training dolphins or swimming with manatees right from the start. But life doesn't work that way. You have to work hard and earn your chances.

She never bought into the whole volunteerism thing.

She never bought into any of it and became miserable once again.

Finally one day when I came home from work a few minutes later than she expected, she blurted it out.

"I can't stand this anymore," she said. "I want a divorce."

The fear in me was gone.

"Yes," I replied. "Let's get divorced."

There I had said it, the words I should have uttered five years earlier. Better late than never.

Of course, once I said that, she changed her tune. In fact, all that night she begged me to change my mind. She said she had spoken too hastily, but I'm the kind of person who sometimes takes a long time to make up my mind. I deliberate. I consider options. I detest confrontation. But once I do make up my mind then that's it.

There was no going back.

In fact, just saying the words: "Yes, we should get divorced," seemed so freeing. My children were crying but I knew this was the right thing. This marriage had run its course. The environment of negativity was not good for the kids. I knew in the long run it would be better for them to stop seeing their father being browbeaten.

I moved in with another reporter at the paper, Alan Snel, and paid him a nominal fee for one of his spare bedrooms. I started seeing my children for overnight visits every Tuesday, Thursday, and every other weekend. I lived on ramen noodles and hot dogs but somehow made it through.

Unfortunately, even though she eventually remarried, what followed was years of bad blood that followed our contentious divorce. To this day she hates me for giving her what she asked for: a divorce.

Luckily, my newfound freedom would eventually lead me to the love of a lifetime and back into the waiting arms of someone I had neglected for so long, God.

FIVE

OVER THE NEXT few years I met two people that would have a tremendous impact on my life.

I continued to work at the newspaper, honing my skills and better learning my craft. I filled in as an editor on the metro desk when needed and continued to draw the most interesting and prestigious assignments.

I did ride-alongs with the Brevard County Sheriff's Office as they conducted raids complete with flash-bang grenades, M-16s, and bulletproof vests. One day I rode with a SWAT team as they executed a series of search-and-arrest warrants on some drug dealers in a dangerous part of South Melbourne near University Avenue. The officers warned me about the disorienting effect of the flash-bang grenades and told me exactly when they would be exploding them.

Still, the moment they went off, I nearly wet my pants and became instantly disoriented. What followed was a foot chase leaving me still dazed and confused alone at a police cruiser. I'm wearing a bulletproof vest and look like I'm a cop. Of course I'm not wearing a gun. So I find myself all alone as a group of angry dangerous-looking men start pointing at me and walking toward the cruiser.

This is generally a neighborhood where the police and the citizens have a contentious relationship. I couldn't even identify myself because they probably hate reporters more than they hate cops. Finally, as they neared, I tried looking as brave as I could. I pumped out my chest, sneered, stared directly at them, then I slammed the cruiser door shut and ran!

You don't realize just how many pounds you need to lose until you are running from an angry mob wearing a heavy bulletproof vest and carrying a video camera. The sweat formed on my body instantly and by the time I was safe enough to stop running, it looked as if someone had unloaded a supersoaker water gun on me.

Finally, I met up with the officers who had used a Taser to subdue their suspect and I felt safe once again. Later that afternoon, feeling a bit more secure, I went into a little grocery store, wearing my vest, for a bottle of water.

"You guys are busy out here today, huh?" the lady behind the counter commented.

Then, in the best police officer voice I could muster, I looked her square in the eye and said: "Ma'am, we're just trying to keep honest, hard-working folks like you, safe."

I did stories about children stricken with cancer, families who lost their teenage children to careless driving, and families desperate for police to solve the murders of their loved ones. I started getting the reputation at the newspaper of being the "tragedy writer," having the stomach to deal with people who have just gone through the most terrible thing that would ever happen in their lives.

It affected me, but in a good way. I began to appreciate my life and the health of my children in ways that I had not before. It was about this time that my editor asked me if I was interested in moving from the Palm Bay bureau—where I sort of made my own hours, wore shorts and flip-flops—to the main office. When I told him that I would think about it, that's when I understood that the request was not really a request. It was a "Godfather" moment, an offer I couldn't refuse.

So I took the collared shirts and neckties out of the closet and started dressing for work in the main office of *Florida Today* in Melbourne. Once again, though I didn't see it at the time, God must have been looking out for me. It's amazing, actually, how faithfully He has taken care of me.

Because it was there, in the Melbourne office that I met Jennifer, the love of my life. I was first introduced to Jennifer during a writing workshop. She was a business reporter who was as beautiful as she seemed quiet. In fact, she stayed silent throughout the entire workshop until the last few minutes.

When she spoke I was blown away by her intelligence and the confidence in her voice. I didn't waste much time finding out that she was single, divorced like me, and with two kids. We hit it off almost instantly and started seeing each other.

Being a journalist herself, Jennifer encouraged me to work late when I had to, to chase the big stories, and to love my craft the way I was intended to. She read every word I wrote and displaced my father as my biggest fan. If a travel opportunity arose, she supported me fully in my work.

We started a serious relationship and after a few months decided to let our children meet. We decided a good family movie, like *Kangaroo Jack* would do the trick. This way the kids could meet and not feel forced into speaking or making immediate friends. But that's just what happened. Fueled by little snack bags of sugary snacks that Jennifer prepared, the kids hit it off immediately. And the sugar fuel? Well that almost got us thrown out of a Wendy's hamburger stop after the movie when the kids could not stop running around the empty restaurant yelling and playing games. It looked like we had the possible makings of a new blended family. Jennifer and I moved in together and we arranged our schedules so that the kids would be together at the same time, allowing us to also have some much-needed alone time a few nights a week.

Three of the kids were only a year apart and my son, the oldest, was about five years older than anyone else. Jennifer and I were so proud of how we handled the manner in which we slowly brought the kids together and made them feel loved and welcomed. We were quite proud of ourselves.

Then we went to Sea World.

Talk about being forced to eat a bit of humble pie! Wow, the kids were still relative strangers and just about everything that could go wrong did that day. My 7-year-old daughter, Jackie, suddenly became very jealous and started holding my hand and pulling me away from Jennifer and the others. My son was quiet and withdrawn. Her kids started pulling away from me in response to jealousy and insecurity that their biological father was instilling in them.

When we got home that night, everyone was in a bad mood. But Jennifer smiled at me and said something comforting about the long road ahead and how all this would just take time.

Knowing she was right, and knowing how madly in love with her I was, I soon asked her to marry me. But, of course, when God is not central to your life, when God is not the focus, things can get much harder.

Before we could even sign the contract with a caterer, Jennifer found out that she was pregnant.

While most people would consider adding another child to the mix a simple blessing from God, you have to remember that I had spent years running from God. And though I did not know it, He was gaining on me.

I didn't want a baby. I was just starting a new relationship and life with the other four kids was challenging enough. Pampers? Formula? You've got to be kidding.

As a born and raised Catholic, I knew abortion was wrong. But, it is painful to say now, I was torn about what I wanted my future wife to do. I tried to be supportive but I'm sure she could sense that I was less than excited about the prospects of being responsible for another life.

But God sent Jennifer into my life for a reason and that reason would not be to kill a child that was conceived in pure and lasting love.

See? Once again God made sure that I did not make a terrible mistake.

Jennifer and I got married secretly at the courthouse while on our lunch break. We went right back to work as man and wife and finished filing our stories. Pretty soon, named after my grandmother "Mamita," Isabelle Mary Torres would be born.

And sure, our private moments were no longer that private and restful nights were interrupted by soiled pampers, wails of hunger, and general baby inconveniences. Still we were thrilled with our new addition to the family, one that has more nicknames—ranging from princess to monster. Isabelle is a part-time challenge and a fulltime joy.

The other day, I asked her if she would draw something in a journal for our church, Holy Name of Jesus Catholic Church in Indialantic. Every week the church allows a family to take home the "Elijah Cup," the chalice used during mass. The family places the chalice in a prominent place and together, the family prays for vocations to religious life. But we also pray for people to just stop and listen to what God is calling them to do.

Anyway, along with the chalice, is a journal. Families are asked to make an entry, share their thoughts. I loved reading what the other families had to write, how much and how hard they prayed.

My experience was a little different. I had a tough time that week with various issues, what I like to call real life, and I felt as if I drew strength from the chalice. Instead of me praying, I felt as if the chalice was there to help me.

Anyhow, I shared that in the journal and then asked Isabelle, who at this moment is nicknamed "Chavs," to draw a picture of the chalice in the journal. She agreed. So I sat her at the kitchen table, placed the gorgeous chalice in front of her and brought her box of crayons.

About 30 minutes later, my precious six-year-old brought me a drawing of the chalice complete with Jesus on the cross, mourning Mary watching, and an angel flying overhead. I saw something dropping from the angel and asked what it was.

"The angel is crying, daddy," she said. "She's crying because Jesus is dying."

This is my precious Isabelle, the child I wasn't sure about keeping, the one I wouldn't trade for anything in this world.

Jennifer left the newspaper after Isabelle was born and started a successful career as a freelance writer. I stayed at the paper and continued to get plum assignments. I also continued writing children's books for a variety of publishers.

I wrote about rap artists, singers, and sports stars. It never made me rich and famous but it provided vacation and Christmas money.

I was happily married with a great wife, wonderful family, and a job that I loved. Of course, I still did not have God in my life but the big man upstairs was working on that. In fact, I'm sure it was no coincidence that a June 2004 phone call was transferred to me.

The voice on the other end belonged to a Titusville businessman by the name of Joe Hurston.

This guy was as aggressive as a used car salesman at the end of the month and almost so pushy that it turned me off. But always having had the yearn to travel—actually yearn is not a strong enough word—my ears perked up when he said he was flying down to the town of Jimani on the border between Haiti and the Dominican Republic. There was room on his Cesna 402 for one more person.

There had been heavy rains and a devastating flashflood. Apparently thousands of people were already dead, many more missing. Joe said he was a former missionary pilot who lived in Haiti for more than 20 years. He wanted to bring two water purifiers down there on a quick 36-hour mission of mercy.

"I haven't done missionary work in years," Hurston told me.

"What's making you get back to it?"

"Well," he laughed, "have you ever heard of the Tuskegee Airmen?"

Of course I had heard of the historic and heroic all-black squadron of World War II fighter pilots. But what on earth could they have to do with this story, a flood on the island of Hispaniola?

"One of those airmen," he continued, "Judge Robert Decatur, lives close by. We're good friends and he called me first thing this morning. He told me that he went to bed last night watching news reports on TV about the floods. He had a tough time sleeping and then was awakened in the middle of the night. He said God had tapped him on the shoulder and told him to do something about the flooding victims."

I took down the information and was intrigued more with every detail Joe offered up. Decatur was apparently one of the real-life Tuskegee Airmen who was the inspiration for the character played by Laurence Fishburne in the movie *The Tuskegee Airmen*. We would land in Santo Domingo and take a pickup truck across the country to the border. Once there, they would provide clean water and deliver donated medications and clothing.

Plus, I would be traveling to Haiti with a living piece of history.

They would be leaving in two days and wanted me to come along! Then Hurston nearly burst my bubble when he asked if I had a passport. At that time you didn't need one to go in and out of Mexico, but Haiti was a different story.

"You absolutely need a passport if you want to come on the trip," he said. "John, let me tell you something. As a journalist, you will make yourself so much more valuable to your employers if you have a passport."

"But you leave in two days," I answered. "There is no way I can get one."

"OK, listen and listen carefully," Joe dug in sensing the sale. "You need to get up bright and early tomorrow and drive down to Miami. They can issue your passport in one day if there is some urgency. I'm telling you, this will be one of the best decisions you can make."

I thought about it for 30 seconds and then went to go tell my editor that I needed the next day to go get my passport.

Two days later I met Joe Hurston for the first time. Little did I know that he would one day lead me back to the Lord. Little did I know just how far that tap from God on the old judge's shoulder would reverberate, touching people for generations to come.

Of course, I didn't see it that way right then and there. In fact, I thought Joe was, well, to be nice, I thought he was strange. He had this serious look on his face at all times, like he was late for a meeting with the president, and his large, bulging eyes looked like they could fix intently on someone and change that person's mind. I tried not to make too much eye contact.

Oh, and he liked to pray.

I've seen people pray. But I've never seen anything like this guy.

"Lord God, Lord Jesus we ask you to throw your blanket of protection over us as we embark on this journey. Know that it is for your glory that we leave our families and friends behind to embark on this mission. By the blood of Jesus we ask you to watch over us, bless us every single second of our trip from John's front door, to the airplane and to Haiti and back. Bless us Lord all the way until we walk back into our homes and see our families again. In your name, sweet Jesus, we pray. Amen."

Then he prayed that the tires of the car were safe and would hold up. And he prayed for the engine of the plane and the tailwinds and the clouds and the new sparkplugs and it seemed as if not five minutes would go by before he was praying for something else.

After a while I got used to it and I sort of liked him. Sure, he was quirky but he was intense and I could tell right away that his words and prayers were so much more than just words and prayers. He meant the things he said. He loved the Gospel and he lived it.

The prayers came in handy when I felt my very first gust of

wind in that itsy-bitsy plane. Holy cow! Talk about losing your stomach. I had never flown in a tiny plane before and was on pins and needles the entire way.

Landing in the Dominican Republic was no better. We weren't landing at the main airport but at some little landing strip elsewhere in Santo Domingo. By this time it had started raining and I could hear Joe say "According to the GPS, it should be right here."

We circled lower and lower amid buildings and houses as the rain got stronger. I don't know what I was expecting but the windshield wipers were no different than the ones on my car. I thought planes had something better, something magical that would keep the rain off of us.

Panic began to creep into my heart and I found myself reciting the Lord's Prayer in my head.

"Our Father, who art in heaven…"

"Ah there it is," Joe finally said, and soon we were on the ground.

Then right there, on the tarmac, standing in the light drizzle, Joe asked us to hold hands and form a circle so we could pray. We continued praying as we loaded a pickup truck with supplies and the water purifiers bound for Jimani and that the traffic would not be heavy, that no rocks would slide down the mountains onto the road and that we could make our way safely to those who needed help.

The drive was many hours and I sat pretty much in silence listening to Joe and the others speak. I knew about a lot of things, different things, but none of it seemed to fit into these conversations. They spoke of hungry people and poverty, about little miracles that occurred on a daily basis and of course, the constant struggle that people in a developing nation had to face daily. This was a place where children still died from diarrhea and where mosquitoes still spread malaria. I had no idea.

As we neared the border with Haiti it felt almost as if

someone was slowly leaking the colors out of our view. It was like one of those movies that switches magically from black and white into color except we were doing it in reverse. The trees started thinning out and green fields became replaced with brown and gray.

We stopped the truck to look at a stone bridge that had been washed away by the flash floods. I snapped some photos and walked down to take a closer look. Joe and the judge were pointing at something and shaking their heads. A pair of children's shoes were lying amid the rubble.

I knew what that meant. We got back in the truck and drove another few minutes to the main part of town, or at least where the town used to be. It looked now like a town of ghosts. There were people everywhere, wandering, or rummaging through the piles of twisted metal, rock, and wood that used to be their homes.

They all shared the same thing in common: an unfocused, dazed look. They were going through the motions, acting like they were living, breathing creatures. But I could see through that. I could see that many of them had lost so much, maybe too much.

We got out and walked around among the ghosts. We found three Haitian brothers, in their early 20s, who agreed to let me interview them. Joe, who speaks perfect Creole, would translate.

The flood sounded like thunder or a train, they explained. It was fast, too fast to really do anything but try and get out of their home. It was the middle of the night and they had been sleeping. Everyone scrambled, no one could see in the dark. It was terrifying. The brothers managed to find each other after the waters had passed. Their home was gone and so were their parents.

They had spent the last few days looking for their mother and father. They had nothing, no money, no food, no jobs, no house, no parents. Their dark faces were as dusty as the collection of rags they wore for clothes.

Their eyes were wide, more yellow than white and as bloodshot as you could get.

"Joe, ask them what they are going to do, how are they going to survive?" I said. "Ask them how do they go on after something like that has happened?"

Joe spoke to them in Creole for a long time and they responded. Then he pulled a few dollars from his wallet and gave it to them.

We started walking back toward the truck. Joe had tears in his eyes and so I waited a moment to get the answers to my questions.

"Did they ask you for money?" I finally asked.

"No, no," he answered with a sad smile forming.

"What are they going to do?" Now the curiosity in me was building up a head of steam.

"They're going to be all right," he answered.

"Well, what did they say exactly, so I can use it in my story," I was trying to sound as if I wasn't losing patience.

"They said," Joe stopped walking and looked me in the eye, "they said they were going to be all right because God would take care of them. They said now, more than ever, they would have to rely on the mercy and love of Jesus Christ."

We walked back to the truck in silence and I couldn't help but be amazed with their faith and dedication even through this tragic disaster. I tried imaging what my reaction would have been and it shamed me to know that I would not have been talking about God.

The reality was that I would have likely been cursing my fate and crying about my future.

We went to the main part of town and distributed some clothing and supplies that we had. That was my first experience with how dangerous a desperate group of people can be. Once word was out that we were there, the people came from all sides, hands open and arms outstretched. It didn't matter what we were there to give them, they wanted some. The crowds pressed in faster and faster until we were left with little choice but to simply drop the bags of used clothing, shoes, toys, and food on the ground and run for our truck. I stayed the longest, taking photographs and scribbling into my notepad. But it wasn't long before people started pulling at me, putting their hands on me and my camera.

It was time to go.

The people clawed and scratched at the supplies while we rode off. We stopped and prayed with a few stragglers, including one man who was badly injured. He lost his daughters in the flood and his swollen eyes looked as if they'd burst if just one more tear escaped. Someone from the group looked at his leg wound and left him some antibiotics.

Joe eventually left the two water purifiers with a missionary who was living close to the region. He would be charged with delivering clean water to the people.

I took more photographs and interviewed more survivors. After a while the stories all have the same sad ring to them. I guess that's the thing about disasters like this when everyone is forced to experience the same terrible event. I had enough photos and information to write a great story for the newspaper and couldn't wait to get back to a place where I could start putting my thoughts down on paper.

We got back in the truck and Joe thanked me for going to Miami and getting my passport on such short notice.

"Jesus sent you John," he said, his soft brown eyes showing just a little bit of wear and tear on them. "You may not know it yet, but He sent you here for a reason. God bless you John Torres."

That night we stopped for dinner at a pizzeria on the road back to Santo Domingo and the judge, an original Tuskegee Airman, regaled us for hours with stories of combat, heroism, and racism. He told us this trip was an "old soldier's last hurrah."

I looked at him closely. He was 84 years old, well off, enjoying his Florida retirement and he decides to come here for a last hurrah. He didn't look a day over 70, though there were some issues. His big burly frame was hunched over to compensate for a multitude of bulging disks, and age had turned his blue eyes grey, like a tired moray eel, one that needs its food chewed up and then brought to him. His ears were made worthless years ago and so he'd squint hard as if that could help his hearing.

He was part of a patrol that sank a German battleship with just machine gun fire. He also helped knock two German jets from the sky.

The judge started telling us about the only time in his life that he ever cried.

First, Joe ordered us all some beer and I liked him even more than before. The pizzeria seemed to grow quiet as the judge started telling his story in his gravelly voice.

"There were four of us, four new officers," he started before taking a small sip. "We were leaving Louisiana and were on our way to Atlanta. We were to be brought up the coast from Atlanta to Fort Meade, which was a huge staging area for overseas deployment—brand new officers, proud of our shining gold bars and wings and all that. I was senior officer by one month, so they had given me all the travel orders and meal vouchers and such from the War Department."

"We boarded the train and started heading toward Alabama. At about 5:30 that evening, the other guys said let's go eat. I had these orders, which called for dining car privileges. Now, we had never eaten in the dining cars before and I thought that maybe it had been a mistake. But here they were, in my hand, and we were going to use them. These boys had never eaten anything fancy, you know, so they were all fired up about it. So, the four of us marched into the dining car and the steward—a black fella—I'll never forget, he said, 'Come in gentlemen. You look so nice and I'm very proud of you.' We came in and we were smiling at the white officers and the civilians who smiled back. Then he sat us down and as soon as he did that he pulled a curtain around us, separating us from the other passengers. That was the most humiliating experience I ever had in my life. It was like they were separating lepers. I put my face in my hands and I cried."

I looked at Joe, whose teary eyes were fixed on the judge.

"I cried man. I tell you I cried. So then I reached up and grabbed the curtain and I snatched it back and I said no way, no, no, uh-uh. Everybody in that dining car fell silent. I will never forget that. You could hear a pin drop. Here we are, officers of the United States Army, I announced to them. We are on our way to overseas duty and possible death fighting for this country. I am not going to put up with this. Well, I looked up and the steward, I saw him from the corner of my eye. I saw him and I turned to look at him and he was standing there crying. Tears, big tears, like the summer rain kind of tears were just falling from his eyes onto his face and onto the tray he was holding. He couldn't even look at me when he apologized over and over again and said there was nothing he could do. I felt sorry for that boy. It wasn't his fault. I put my hand on his back and I told him we were going back up into that Jim Crow car, which was up front in front of the coal car. We went up there and sat and just waited. None of us spoke."

"Anyways, we sat there drinking cheap whiskey for about an hour and a half and all of a sudden here come the waiters with every kind of food they had, plates of pheasant, turkey, pot roast and crawfish. They also brought over a bottle of good whiskey and a bucket full of beers. You name it and it was there at our fingertips. They came in dancing and that black steward, the one with the grapefruit-sized tears, he was leading the way. He looked so happy and so proud. 'This is for you,' he said. 'We are all so proud of you.' And he served us and danced and sang songs from his father. My eyes watered again and I'll tell you, I don't think I ever tasted food that tasted as good as that night. That happened in 1944 and I will never forget it."

I smiled at the judge and clinked my beer bottle with his. I knew I would always remember every single word of that story. I wrote a story for *Florida Today* in 2009 when he passed away.

Joe Hurston spoke at the funeral.

I'm so grateful that God decided to tap the judge on the shoulder.

SIX

I STAYED IN touch with Joe after our trip to the ravaged border area between Haiti and the Dominican Republic. I also wrote a few more stories over the months about his relief efforts in Haiti and the fundraising he was doing to fund the water purifiers and the mission work. Joe made my job easy because he enjoyed being in the newspaper! I'm poking a little fun there, I know that he looks at the press as a way to try and raise money for the mission work and, in some cases, to spread the word of God.

Plus, I liked him. I honestly did. Though I knew there was not a whole lot we had in common and I knew that his relationship with God was on a whole different level. We'd even spoken on the telephone a few times just to say hello.

In a way, I always expected Joe to give me the sales pitch, you know, the whole conversion speech. The "why aren't you close to God" guilt-trip. But he never did. No, and in fact, one of the things I admired about him was that he never seemed to openly try and evangelize. Sure, he wanted and still wants everyone to convert and accept Jesus. But he let his actions, his relief work, his love, do the evangelizing for him.

Looking back now, I think he infused me with Jesus through osmosis.

My journey with Joe Hurston would take a much deeper path a few months later, when a cataclysmic earthquake rocked the bottom of the Indian Ocean on the day after Christmas 2004. When I saw the headlines that the death toll would likely reach the hundreds of thousands, I thought it would be the perfect place for him to put his water purifiers to good use.

That Christmas Eve, Jennifer and I went to church and it was nice. I liked the peaceful atmosphere and how so many of the people seemed to know each other. Having to share the children from our first marriages with our former spouses, we normally have one set until 1 p.m. Christmas Day and then the other set arrives shortly after.

I've tried to make and keep Christmas as special and memorable as my parents did for my sisters and me. We bake cookies or pies, make special meals—like Jennifer's special apple wontons—watch just about every Christmas movie ever made, decorate the house, and then really take our time opening gifts on Christmas morning.

We do it just the way my dad did when I was a child. I get down on my knees at tree level and call out who the gift is for. We go around and around until there are no more presents. I love that the children seem to have picked up on the generosity at Christmas and how great it feels to be able to see someone you love open a present that you bought for them.

My daughter Jackie, in particular, uses money and gift cards she receives for her birthday a few weeks before Christmas to buy Christmas presents for her friends and family.

That is something that makes me proud.

I called Joe on the phone after seeing worsening reports of the situation in Thailand, Indonesia, and parts of the Indian coast. I wished him a Merry Christmas, exchanged pleasantries, and then asked him when we were leaving for Indonesia.

One week later, I was part of a group of seven people—including Emmy-award winning documentarian John Goheen, who met Joe a few months earlier when the hurricanes ravaged Haiti—who found ourselves on a commercial airplane to the worst natural disaster in our history.

Once again, Jennifer supported my decision to go right from the start. Even when my editors at the newspaper balked at me going, she said I should take a week's worth of vacation time and just go. So I did. She sacrificed a week of time off that we could spend together. She put my needs to report on this story and follow the truth ahead of her needs and worries. She would spend the next week worried sick about not being able to reach me as I traveled to the largest Muslim country in the world, not knowing if we would even have a place to sleep.

The decision to go was made a bit easier by the fact that I had made a deal with my former newspaper, the *Poughkeepsie Journal*, to send a story or two and to write a pair of children's books for one of the publishers that fed me steady work.

The trip went something like this: Orlando to New York to Hong Kong for a night—then on to Jakarta for two nights before catching a flight to Medan on Sumatra.

Plagued with a bad back, I took a sleeping pill when we took off from New York's Kennedy Airport hoping that the 15-hour flight would pass quickly. And it worked, my lids grew heavy shortly after reaching altitude, then I was off to la-la land. I slept and I dreamt and I slept some more. When I woke, I wiped the sleep from my eyes, and tried focusing on the board at the front of the plane that showed the plane's route and how much time was left. Maybe we would almost be there!

I looked, I peered, I stared and, and, and only 13 hours and 26 minutes left in the flight! What? I have never been on such a long flight and it felt even longer. At least every seat was equipped with its own on-demand menu of movies and television shows to pass the time. I watched a few movies but I also spent a lot of time alone with my iPod. I remember how much strength I drew from the song "My City of Ruins," by Bruce Springsteen.

"With these hands, with these hands, I pray Lord, pray for the strength Lord, pray for the faith Lord and pray for the love Lord," he sang over and over into my ear buds.

It was during that flight, and without even consulting my better half Jennifer, that I asked Joe Hurston if he would stand up for my daughter Isabelle as godfather for her baptism.

What better model could I ask for? What better spiritual

guide? He would be able to provide her with the spirituality that I knew I could not. He was moved and accepted immediately. Jennifer and I waited until Isabelle was 18 months old to have her baptized as God was not at the forefront of our lives.

"I'd be honored to, John," he said, his eyes growing just a little misty. "When is her birthday?"

Over the years I've learned not to believe in coincidences. I believe that God has a plan for all of us and things, everything, happens for a reason. I was nowhere close to thinking this way yet in life though I was blown away by the incredible "coincidence" that both Isabelle and Joe Hurston shared the birthdates of January 13!

We all felt that sort of *Twilight Zone* chill when we realized they had the same birthday.

The rest of the flight was uneventful and we landed in Hong Kong where we spent the night. I called Jennifer and e-mailed her from a small restaurant where I had a bowl of the best fried rice imaginable. Since we had an early flight in the morning to Jakarta, we were able to leave the 20 water purifiers and battery packs at the airport.

Despite the early flight, I wandered around Hong Kong until the early morning hours with the guy I was bunking with—Chris Stamper—and Joe's daughter, Cherie. We walked around, strolled into shops and conversed with strangers.

It was a great night.

During the flight to Jakarta I was mentally preparing myself for the disaster that I would soon witness. I did not realize that Indonesia is made up of thousands of islands and that Jakarta suffered no damage at all. In fact, we stayed at a pretty swanky hotel for two nights trying to figure out our next move.

It was hard to find evidence anywhere at all that this country was smack dab in the middle of one of the worst natural catastrophes in history. However, a few people at the hotel did approach us and thank us for coming to their country to help them. They shook our hands, smiled and bowed slightly.

Joe spent his time on the phone and met with different people trying to find the best route he could to the disaster site. It would not be so easy. Finally, the decision was made to hop a flight to the island of Sumatra and stage out of Medan. It was still a good way from the ground zero point but at least we would now be on the same island.

The flight to Sumatra was very crowded with locals, many carrying boxes, parcels or huge carry-on bags in their laps. I sat with a burly, round-faced man whose eyes were swollen. I was tired and am not usually one to talk with strangers on a plane, but I think I may have been the first American he ever met.

He was intent on striking up a conversation, starting off by asking if I was English. When I corrected him and said no, American, his eyes lit up.

"Why? Why are you here?" he asked in surprisingly good English.

"To help, you know, with the tsunami," I answered, as if it wasn't obvious enough.

Then the round-faced man grabbed my hand and started shaking it. I could see that he was starting to get emotional. He began talking in his native language to many of the other passengers around us. They started smiling at me and patting me on the shoulder. I felt quite proud of myself.

Then I asked him if he lived in Sumatra, was he going home?

No, he answered, he was going to the city of Meulaboh, where the tsunami had washed nearly everything away.

Excitedly, I told him that was where we were going as well, eventually. He scribbled his address down and several phone numbers for me to contact him there. Then I asked him why he was going there.

"To look for my daughter," he responded, the smile vanishing from his face. She had been missing since the giant wave of water came crashing down on the city.

I didn't know what to say. I put my hand on his arm as tears streamed down his face. His grandkids were missing too.

At his insistence, we posed for a photo together at the stifling hot airport in Medan, a grimy, dark city where many of the military and relief organizations had gathered and set up bases shortly after the tsunami. I shook his hand goodbye and wished him luck.

I will never know if he found his daughter, but judging from what I would see over the next few days, I'd have to say the chances were remote.

The hotel in Medan was starkly different from the opulence we enjoyed in Jakarta. This looked like something from the 1940s with ornate furnishings and a ballroom type lobby. Stairs went up on both sides and you could walk completely around the lobby and look down from the landing above.

The scene was surreal. It looked as if it could have come directly out of a movie. There were soldiers everywhere you looked, coming from different directions and heading in different directions. It was as if someone had choreographed this strange ballet of German, Japanese, Italian, Spanish, American, English, and Singaporean servicemen and women. Everyone was in a hurry and no one ever smiled.

Then, every afternoon, at the center of this orchestrated chaos, a stunningly beautiful Chinese woman with hair falling down to her lower back, and dressed as if going to the prom, would sit at the piano and perform the most beautifully sad classical pieces she knew.

It was really quite the scene.

The hotel had no Internet service or working telephones so there was no way to reach Jennifer and the kids. I did warn her of this previously and hoped that she would not be worrying too much. But, of course, I knew she would be.

After a day of trying to figure out what our next move would be, the team was faced with a choice. It seemed everyone at that hotel was trying to get to ground zero to assist and transportation was a severely limited commodity. We found a truck that would basically drive us to Meulaboh or Banda Aceh but because of the state of the roads, it would likely be an 18-hour journey.

We decided to pass, spend one more night in Medan, and see if any other opportunities presented themselves.

So, filmmaker John Goheen and I chose to spend the day at a refugee camp, talking with and interviewing some of the people who survived the tsunami. I found a very good guide, someone who could speak several languages as Indonesia is home to many different nationalities.

We arrived at the camp and the first thing I saw were people gathered around a very long bulletin board. With the images of the missing from the terrorist attacks of 9-11 still fresh in my mind, I knew from a distance what they were looking at. Still, one could not help but be moved and filled with pity at the site of thousands of photographs of missing loved ones.

This, it turns out, was a Chinese refugee camp. I had no idea that Indonesia had such a large population of Chinese people. Many were crying, consoling each other. Others cooked rice in pots meant to feed entire armies. Children were playing with toys constructed from plastic plates or other bits of trash. Men talked loudly and smoked cigarettes. Some slept atop giant bags of rice.

My translator explained things to me, but he didn't have to. Anyone with eyes or a heart could see the emotional suffering going on here. Then, I spotted a woman with short hair in a yellow dress who was crying, uncontrollably. No, it was more than that, she was wailing to the heavens as if pleading with God to please take her as well.

I asked my translator if we could go speak with her. After all, I was under contract to send a story to the *Poughkeepsie Journal* newspaper and to write a pair of children's books on the disaster.

He hesitated and I asked again.

Finally, he shook his head no. My initial reaction was anger but immediately reasoned with myself that he was not a professional journalist, he was simply a guy who was willing to help me out a bit.

We kept wandering around the camp and I took notes and photos. I was amazed by how the little children were so beautifully dressed in very expensive clothing amid all this misery. A short while later, my translator grabbed my arm and led me to the woman who was still crying.

He agreed to help me get the interview.

The woman was still crying and sipping from a bottle of water when we went into a small break room and sat at a table. I wrote frantically while the translator relayed her story.

She was home with her husband and three-year-old son when the ground began shaking. Everything fell off the walls and it sounded like bombs going off. Not knowing what to do, she and her husband grabbed the child and ran outside just in case the house collapsed.

It shook for a long time while they stood outside and it was hard for them to keep their balance. Finally, it stopped and there was damage everywhere out on the street. The husband said he needed to go check on his elderly parents and sent his wife and child back inside.

Everything seemed OK, the worst was over.

But only moments after her husband took the motor scooter to check on his parents, the woman was startled by a loud banging on her door. It was the police and they were yelling for her to leave the house and flee.

"The water is coming," they yelled. "The water is coming."

She did not know what that meant exactly but rushed outside to see hundreds of people running inland away from the ocean.

She started running and without looking behind her she could soon hear the water crashing through the city. Before long she was running in the water as it surged past her and started rising higher and higher from her ankles to her knees to her waist.

When the rushing water became too strong for her she moved to a street corner and started clinging to a wooden utility pole. She told her little boy that it would be all right and that they would be safe. But the water kept rising and more and more people arrived to share the same utility pole.

The woman stopped telling her story for a moment and took a sip of water. Then she put her face in her hands and wept for a few moments before trying to continue. I felt like a complete and utter jerk but I took my camera out of its case and snapped her photo. Inside, I knew I probably should have put an arm around her or touched her hand with mine. Instead, I took her photograph as she told me about the worst moment in her life.

It was getting harder and harder to hold onto her child. Now there was barely any room to hold onto the pole and the surging water was getting stronger and more violent. Someone being carried by the water's seemingly endless flow came careening toward the pole and knocked into the woman as he grabbed on for his life.

Her baby, her three-year-old son, was jarred loose from her arms.

She yelled and tried to go after him but the others at the utility pole held her back as she would surely drown. She watched in vain as her little boy's head bobbed under the water five times before he stayed under for good.

"Mama," he cried each time his little head broke the surface. "Mama."

I told my translator to tell her how sorry I was that this happened. And I asked her if she found her husband.

The husband searched frantically for his parents but never found them. When he finally found his wife, the look on his face was enough to tell him what had happened. He fell to his knees with his arms outstretched toward the heavens and screamed.

They were the lucky ones, they actually found their son's body a little later. There were thousands more who had no body to bury, no closure.

I was shaken by this woman's story. In the matter of a few short moments her family's life was altered forever. Her son and her in-laws were gone forever. I started thinking about the moments right before the earthquake struck. I wished I had asked her what they were doing. Were they singing together? Maybe they were playing a family game or reading a book. What was the last thing they said together before the earthquake?

I couldn't get the mental picture of the little boy bobbing up and down in the water out of my head for the rest of the day. For the rest of the afternoon I said little as we toured the rest of the camp in the stifling heat.

We returned to the hotel around 6 p.m. and learned that Joe had yet to secure a ride for us to get closer to the disaster site. He was a little feverish from travel and stress and did not look well at all. The plan was for everyone to meet for dinner after freshening up but I never made it.

Traumatized by that woman's story and haunted by the image of her son's last few moments of life, I went to bed. It was still light out.

I woke to the phone ringing shortly after 7 in the morning. I had slept 13 straight hours! I felt better but I still could not understand how God could let something like this happen. The problem was that I was really in no position to question God since we really did not have a relationship.

Anyhow, Joe was calling an emergency meeting in his room. When we got there he looked so much better. Like me, it appeared as if he needed a full night of rest to recuperate from the trip and, it seemed, to prepare for the things we would soon see.

He told us that the Holy Spirit had planted an idea in his head while he slept. We would set up a water purifier right in the lobby of the hotel, alongside the long-haired piano-playing Chinese woman and surely someone with the means to get us to ground zero would be interested enough to take us.

Surely Joe was a man of faith. He had no doubt that a plan inspired by the Holy Spirit could possibly fail. If he did have a doubt he was sure masking it pretty well. I on the other hand was figuring the closest I would ever get to the tsunami site was to tour more refugee camps. I could still write a great story. I had started attending the media briefings at the hotel for updates on rescue, mortality rates, and relief efforts.

Still, I was disappointed that we would not be making it to the point of impact.

We all helped Joe with buckets of water and creating a nice display of water purifiers and their battery packs. Meanwhile, Joe set up a purifier atop a table he commandeered and started purifying water from one of the buckets.

Now, the purifier uses an ultraviolet light source that glows a pleasing purple, bluish light. With the water running through it, the machine looks like a pretty cool gadget. Before long, soldiers from several different countries were stopping, staring, asking questions, and chatting it up with Joe. Like moths drawn to the light, they continued to arrive, sometimes creating crowds around us. The Spaniards were interested, the Australians were curious, the Americans were ambivalent, but it was the Singaporeans who invited Joe to show his purifier to a group of upper-tier military men in a closed door meeting.

He emerged beaming, but only praising the Holy Spirit who had made it all happen.

"Pack a bag, a very, very light bag," he said. "We can only take so much weight with us in the morning when we board the helicopter!"

I was definitely impressed. The hotel in Medan was loaded with people who wanted to get closer to the disaster and we, Joe, had done it in only a few days. That night, after a few gin and tonics at the hotel bar, I went to my room to write a story of my experiences so far. Gin and tonic is normally my drink of choice when traveling. Someone once told me that tonic contains the same ingredient—quinine—that is in anti-malaria medications. I don't know if the gin and tonics help, but I've yet to contract the disease despite the numerous mosquito bites encountered.

My old newspaper, the *Poughkeepsie Journal*, would be running my piece on Sunday's opinion page as a guest columnist. They were interested in just about anything I could send, as long as I could send it while still in Indonesia.

I knew there was probably no way I would be able to file a story from Meulaboh if the damage was anything close to what I had imagined. I needed to get them the story before morning.

After completing the emotional column detailing my visit to the refugee camp and the man I met on the airplane who was missing his daughter, I tried every possible way to send the story from the hotel but could not. Internet service was spotty at best and it just was not working right now. I enlisted the help of Joe's daughter, Cherie, and one of our travel companions, Chris Stamper.

We took several flights of stairs up to the hotel's roof and then up a separate landing to the helipad. Chris held the open laptop in his arms that was connected to the satellite phone Cherie was holding as far as her outstretched arms could go over her head and I, well I hit the send button.

It was a great moment and we were all quite pleased with ourselves for getting the job done. It was a picture I will never forget.

We were up early the next morning and caught a ride to the airfield, which looked like a war scene with helicopters and planes landing every few seconds. The choppers especially resembled hummingbirds, darting in and out, up and down, performing this ballet.

The wait for our chopper was long. Looking back I think we must have waited four or five hours for the Singaporean soldiers to finally come get us and escort the group to the helipad. The flight was about 90 minutes and they must have made three trips before getting us.

We waited again at the landing pad. It was our group, now reduced to six after one member fell ill, and about a dozen refugees carrying shopping bags and poorly wrapped cardboard boxes. It was one of those moments in life where everything seemed to slow down and get very quiet despite the whir and roar of the helicopters all around. It was as if the body was helping to prepare for what was coming next. I could almost hear the blood pumping through my veins or my own heart beating. It was peaceful and almost nice, though I started to find myself needing to hold back tears that wanted to spring forward.

Then I heard a sound, a very high-pitched sound that was almost like a sad sweeping song except it was worse. One of the women waiting for us on the tarmac had stopped trying to hold back the tears and was letting the pain go. She started crying very softly, her voice trembling into a vibrato. I looked over without staring and could see the anguish in her face. A single tear tumbled slowly down her face, falling a few inches, then pausing before continuing on.

Every one of us ignored her; everyone except for Joe Hurston. He walked over and put his arm around the tiny woman. He held her close and tight in his arms and then she let go. She wailed and moaned and cried as he comforted her, breaking through the barrier of different languages to console her with his hushed tones and understanding eyes.

Following his example, we all moved a little bit closer. I snapped a photo of her in his arms, which hangs on my wall at home today. An Indonesian soldier, who couldn't have been more than 14 years old and who looked as if the rifle he was toting was big enough to fire him, wandered over to see what was going on.

His English was barely good enough to do a little translating for us and that's where we learned that the woman had lost 40 of her closest relatives in the tsunami.

Forty!

Her husband, her children save for one, her cousins, aunts, uncles, parents, all of them were wiped out. The story was the same as the others from the refugee camp—the ground shook followed almost instantly by a rush of water and pandemonium Her little boy, about 10 years old, stood quietly behind with a hint of worry on his face. In all likelihood, he had seen his mother cry like this many times in the past week.

After living in a camp for the better part of a week, they were going home.

Her painful, mournful song was haunting. And I swear that to this day I feel as if I can still hear her crying.

The Chinook helicopter was big, loud, and surprisingly gentle as it touched down, kicking up a swirl of dust around us. Chinooks are those large choppers with two long blades fixed atop and spinning in different directions. I stared and stared trying to figure out how the blades never hit one another.

I started thinking that I probably would feel better on a plane if it was to malfunction because there is always the possibility that the pilot would be able to glide us down to relative safety. But this monstrosity of a helicopter? If something went wrong here, this thing would come spiraling down from the sky. I pictured the blades touching while we were thousands of feet in the air and the whole thing just coming apart.

For the first time on this trip I was a little nervous.

Once the large hatch door on the rear was lowered open, soldiers rushed out and hurried us on. It reminded me of so many scenes from movies where evacuees are rushing to get on a chopper before some disaster occurred or the enemy army approached. But here we were rushing to leave a perfectly safe place to journey toward a disaster. Maybe there was some technical reason for the frantic rush. Maybe operations were simply behind schedule or they needed to save fuel. I don't know what it was but we were all securely on the helicopter within moments of it landing.

I held on to the straps around me with all my might until my knuckles turned a sickly white. But once we were airborne, I was stunned at how smooth the ride was. It didn't even feel as if we were in the air at all.

The wailing woman's son's eyes were fixed on me as I ripped open a protein bar that was in my bag. I tore it open and gave him half. Joe saw the exchange and smiled at me. Then he motioned, with his pursed lips, for me to look at the boy's mother.

She was reading a pocket-sized version of the Quran. The tears had gone and she actually looked up and smiled at us.

Can God really heal someone so quickly? I thought to myself, before closing my eyes and dozing gently to the calming whir of the motors. I guess if the blades were going to touch each other they would have already.

I woke as the helicopter very slowly began to descend from over the mountains we had flown over. The place that used to be the city of Meulaboh was still not visible but I could tell we were near.

My heart panicked and I found myself reciting the "Our Father" and the "Hail Mary" in my head over and over again. I was praying! That was something I had not done in a very long time and I don't know what exactly prompted me to start here. But with every word that passed through my mind, I could feel a strength, a protection, rise up in me.

I can't say for sure, but it looked like several other people on the helicopter were praying for strength as well.

Spotting the city that used to be Meulaboh from the air was not difficult. As the helicopter circled and descended slowly, the concrete block houses that had been reduced to powder were dotted everywhere. In some cases the only things left were the concrete slabs where the homes had been built.

No one said a word as the helicopter landed and we were rushed off as quickly as we were rushed on. A few feet from the landing pad, an open-air truck was waiting to take us to the local base of operations where the Australian military had taken a lead role.

We drove right past the city's main square which resembled a vacant Hollywood lot or scene from some futuristic apocalyptic movie. The tall clock in the square had stopped working and was stuck at the hour of doom for these people. Cars were flipped upside down, boats had landed miles from shore, and buildings were either twisted or destroyed.

There was dust everywhere.

There were no people, no stores, no signs of life anywhere except for rescue crews and military vehicles working to clear the major roads.

Now the group would be staying for about another week but I had only two days before I had to catch my flights home and make it back to the newspaper. Remember, I had done this on my own time and there were some who were not too happy about it.

At the base we inquired about a flight back and the Aussies said the earliest seat on a chopper would be in about 10 days. Panic gripped my heart. Jennifer would be worried sick if I wasn't on the plane and if I was out of communication for that long. Plus, in all likelihood I would be getting fired.

To make matters worse, the Aussies issued a warning that made me question what the heck I was even doing there.

"Stay in groups and on the main roads," the officer told us. "There has been a lot of separatist rebel activity around here lately."

Disaster, no flight home, and now rebels, this was just dandy.

"Don't worry John," Joe said. "We'll get you out of here in time to catch your flights."

The next day and a half were spent exploring the area, providing clean drinking water to the people, taking photos, and interviewing locals. We stayed close to a large muddy field that just became saturated with the flooding. They pulled several bodies from that mud while we were staying there.

The one thing that left a lasting impression on me was how resilient the people were. I wondered if this was a trait of these Indonesians living in Sumatra or would anyone react the same way after going through such a catastrophe.

They were grateful for the help and ready to move on with their lives. They were eager to make friends with us, smile, share their stories, and even laugh. The children especially, even though many had lost parents, siblings, and friends, followed us around and loved mugging for our cameras.

I learned that the only ones who lived were the people lucky enough to run and make it onto higher ground. No animals died, they explained as well. The animals, they said, knew something was going on and immediately started inland looking for elevated areas.

They had lost everything they had but they did not lose hope.

Joe had rented a small house for the team to stay in and I, somehow or other, was able to sleep on this tiny couch that might as well have been made out of rock. But boy did I sleep.

"John Torres, you have the main quality that every true missionary of the Lord must have," laughed Joe. "You can sleep anywhere!"

There was no water or electricity but at least we had a roof over our heads. I was thankful for that.

I had no real hope of catching a flight back to Medan and then Jakarta on the morning I was scheduled to leave but Joe insisted that he would get me out. Then he stopped everything and prayed that I would be able to make all my flights and connections. We drove to the military base and walked across this long grassy field to speak with the Singaporeans about their helicopters.

Now, let me tell you, I live in Florida and have traveled to some pretty warm places. But the heat from the sun in Indonesia was something else entirely. It took all of my strength to walk across that grassy field and by the time I was done I felt as if I could no longer breathe or walk a step farther. It's the kind of heat that just simply zaps everything out of you.

One of our crew, Doug Rodante, must have felt the same way because he collapsed into a chair drawing the attention of the team by how much he was perspiring. We were concerned but felt like laughing at the same time. He looked as if someone had grabbed a garden hose and sprayed him for a full two minutes. That's how wet with sweat he was.

"OK, John," Joe said, as he emerged from speaking with a Singaporean officer, "a seat just opened on the next Chinook. You're going home."

I couldn't believe it. But I should have. Joe prayed for it, had faith it would happen and it did.

There was no time for long goodbyes. I waved to my travel mates and jumped on the chopper. I was coming home.

It didn't matter to me that I would not have time to get clean clothes out of my suitcases or even have time for a shower. I was wearing clothes that I had worn for about three days and I was desperately in need of a hot shower, a change of clothes, and a shave. But I was going back to my family and I missed them all desperately.

I barely made my flights, having to literally run through two airports looking like a refugee myself. Finally, in Tokyo, I was able to reach Jennifer who was relieved to finally hear from me. I told her how much I loved her and missed her and that I would see her before long.

I had about eight hours to kill in the Tokyo airport and so I went shopping for some clothes. There was no place that sold cargo shorts, like the pair I was wearing, and I didn't feel like buying dressy slacks so I stayed with those. But I was able to secure underwear, women's socks, and a brown pullover shirt.

Then, for $5, I was able to rent out a small space that had a bathroom, shower, and couch for 30 minutes. The four-hour rentals were taken. I showered, shaved, and with my new ensemble felt like a different man.

It was only after I sat in the terminal looking at the receipts that I realized I had just spent $120 for that shirt! I had never spent that much for any one piece of clothing and I felt ill. But there was nothing really now to do but laugh. I vowed to wear the shirt once a week until I died to get the usage out of it.

The reunion with Jennifer at Orlando International Airport

was sweet. I missed her more than anything and I was very thankful that God had brought me home safely to someone who loved me so much and who I simply adored.

Everything was good at the newspaper and even the editor, who was annoyed that I had gone, asked me if I would write a story about the trip for the paper. I made a deal and was able to get some of my vacation days back in exchange.

I was extremely emotional in the weeks following my return. Greeting card commercials would make me cry and even certain songs on the radio would get me misty-eyed without me even realizing it. My kids noticed the change as well. I was having a tough time keeping it together.

Then one day I received a call from Doug Rodante, the perspiring guy, to say hello. We had a nice chat and we relived some of the trip's highlights before I learned the true reason for his call.

"John, are you feeling sad lately? I mean really sad, like weepy and stuff?"

"Yes," I answered, and then went through the entire litany of commercials and songs and silly television shows that were getting me all emotional.

"I think that was part of it," he said.

I didn't understand.

"I think part of it, maybe all of it, I think our mission was to go down there and take some of their sadness away from them. I think we had to bring some of it back with us because they had experienced too much of it."

I hung up the phone and realized he was right. And after learning that my sadness was alleviating some of theirs, I felt better.

SEVEN

MY EXPERIENCES traveling to Indonesia, Mexico, and Haiti, and the prize-winning stories I had written, set me up nicely as the newspaper's go-to guy when it came to travel. So it came as little surprise when they asked me if I would like to do a series of stories about the plight of cruise ship workers.

The project entailed a photographer and me taking a four-day cruise to the Bahamas and making enough contacts to try and track where the workers were sending their money. I chose to focus on the Indian workers because they were hardworking, polite, humble, and they spoke English.

The tough thing about focusing on Indians, however, is that they are very private people, and it was very hard to tell if they were being forthcoming with us. The cruise was boring, filled with 50-year-old overweight women looking for love.

It saddened me to learn that over the years the Indian crew members were shifted from the lucrative wait-staff in the restaurants to basically nighttime maintenance and painting. Even though their English skills were best suited for working the food lines and for waiting tables, the cruise lines decided that passengers would rather be waited on by attractive white Eastern Europeans than dark-skinned Indians.

The focus of the story took the photographer and me to Mumbai, India, the city formerly known as Bombay.

I cannot express how utterly excited I was to visit the land of Ghandi and the mysticism of this ancient land. I bought books about the culture and the history to be better prepared. But seriously, nothing could prepare me for the poverty, wretchedness, and utter filth that permeated this city of 14 million.

The stench was evident from the second we set foot off the airplane. During the ride to our hotel, we witnessed several small children foraging through dumpsters for food. It was one o'clock in the morning on a Tuesday! Why were these children out ripping through trash for a meal? That sight put a bad taste in my mouth for the rest of the week that was only exacerbated by the endless smog, the fumes from the three-wheeled auto-rickshaws, the endless crowds of people begging, and those trying to pick your pocket.

More than once we found people trying to unzip our backpacks as we made our way through the crowds. I found the entire experience to be a real let-down and while I am sure India has many, many beautiful and captivating places to visit, I saw none of them during my eight days there.

This is a country with nuclear energy and a thriving economy? This is the country that has produced renowned philosophers, mathematicians, and physicists?

I saw children cooling off in sewage water, rivers that were clogged with trash, and even a boy whipping himself as he walked down the street.

"What is he doing?" I incredulously asked my guide as the boy went seemingly unnoticed by the throngs of people hustling to their destinations.

"Oh nothing," he said, doing that famous headshake from side-to-side, "he is just possessed by the devil."

Possessed by the devil? What kind of place is this?

Every night I would get back to my hotel, my eyes bleary and burning from the pollution and my spirit broken by the things I had seen that day. I'd have a gin and tonic with the photographer in the lobby bar and then go up to my room to call Jennifer. Thank God I had her. I found Mumbai to be a very depressing place and for the first time during my travels, I could not wait to leave and go home.

But every night she would give me the pep talk I needed. Near the end of my trip, I remember being especially discouraged by the day's events. I told her how disappointed I was in the city and how I would have left right then and there if I could have.

But instead of commiserating in my misery, she urged me to look forward to what the next day could bring.

"Make it a point," she said, "to find one beautiful thing or one precious moment tomorrow and enjoy it, really focus on it and hold on to it. That should help."

I had never heard such great advice and it gave me hope that tomorrow would be better.

The next day, armed with a better attitude and a new outlook, I set out to do the last of the reporting I would need to be able to write this series of articles. We visited hiring agencies where people would line up for a chance at one of those elusive cruise ship jobs. We interviewed a man whose career aboard the cruise ships was cut short when he needed open-heart surgery. Now, after working for that one particular line for 17 years, he had retained a lawyer to try and secure disability benefits.

Then, just as dusk started approaching, I found the moment I had been looking for. I was standing on a small bridge overlooking a bay that led out to the Arabian Sea. The sun was nearly done for the day and it was sinking slowly into the dark waters. There were children swimming and splashing around the calm sea and really having a good time. I focused on their smiles and faraway yelps of joy.

I took a deep breath and let out a long, slow sigh. This was it, I thought. Finally, I have discovered some tenderness, some peace, some beauty. Then as I scanned the image from side to side, only yards from where the children were swimming, I saw several men—with their trousers lowered—defecating on the shore.

They were going to the bathroom, number two mind you, at the water's edge as people swam a few feet away. I could simply not believe my eyes. I called the photographer over to make sure he was seeing what I was, and both of us stood there, mouths wide open, not able to speak.

Two days later I was home, safe and sound with my family in our small, but cozy home. Perhaps the ultimate letdown of the trip was when the plane from Mumbai was about to land in Paris for a short layover, the plane's flight attendants went up and down the aisles handing out face masks, the kind surgeons wear so as not to contaminate the operation. Then they sprayed every one of us with bug spray! We were being fumigated and I didn't know whether to laugh or cry.

My project for the newspaper, "Canaveral's Crews" won me several more writing awards, even though I felt it lacked the punch and the impact of "El Sueno." These workers, while perhaps exploited to a degree, were treated infinitely better than any orange picker ever was. While the fruit-pickers of my "El Sueno" project years earlier relied on picking crops for their very survival, these cruise ship workers relied on their work to improve their lot in life.

Only a few months after I returned from Mumbai, I learned that Joe Hurston was on his way there. There had been weeks of terrible rain and the city was flooded. Thousands had been killed and he was going, as he does, to deliver clean water. This guy was tireless and I did not envy him having to go there during even worse conditions than I. But he truly felt that it was his Gospel-appointed duty to go and give cups of clean water in Jesus' name.

"What can be more pure, more simple, more loving than giving water to someone who is thirsty?" he'd ask.

It was while Joe was in India, however, that his home state suffered the greatest catastrophe in American history. Hurricane Katrina pounded New Orleans and the Gulf Coast so harshly that the levees burst and the "Big Easy" was literally under water.

Joe left his wife and fellow "water mules" in Mumbai to continue their relief efforts and he flew around the globe back to

Florida where he would do what he does best—organize relief efforts.

Remarkably, less than 24 hours after that agonizingly long flight from India, Joe had lined up a half-dozen small planes bound for Baton Rouge, the place he was born. As he always does, Joe invited me along and this time I took friend and fellow reporter Wayne Price with me.

We met at the Titusville Airport at four in the morning and I laughed when I saw our plane. It was a Cessna 337, the kind of plane that has a small propeller in the front and one in the back. It is meant really as a personnel transport and there is little room for cargo. That must have explained why it looked as if someone had simply decided to make half a plane.

"Joe, where is the other half of this thing?" I joked, eying this raggedy looking half-plane that seemed about as airworthy as Chitty-chitty Bang-bang.

He assured me it was one of the safer planes out there and so after the usual prayer circle outside the aircraft, we were off. It was an extremely tight fit but somehow or other, among boxes of food, socks, supplies, and battery packs for the water purifiers, I was able to get my body in a position to fall asleep. Like Joe says, I can fall asleep anywhere.

The ride was smooth as there was very little wind. Some of the best weather I have ever seen actually comes on the heels of a hurricane. It's like all the bad air leaves and the good air comes in.

I don't exactly know what time it was but I know that the sun had started rising behind us when Joe woke me to find the satellite phone packed in among supplies in the rear of the plane. There is something about a pilot of a small plane asking you for the emergency phone when you are thousands of feet in the air above the Gulf of Mexico that gets you to wake up in less than an instant.

To Joe's credit he remained as calm as he could while asking his son and copilot to look up the home phone number of the plane's owner. My heart was racing now and I could feel the blood start pulsing in my neck. Somehow my ears were able to silence the roar of the engines on the plane as well as my own rapidly firing heart to hear the conversation between Joe and the man he had just awakened.

In a nutshell, the rear engine had conked out meaning our twin engine plane was now a single engine plane. I found myself once again reciting the "Our Father" in my head along with several "Hail Marys." The Hail Mary is my favorite prayer. I have many Christian friends who don't understand what they call the Catholic obsession with Mary, but I look at it this way. How can you lose when you ask the mother of Jesus to intercede on your behalf? After all, what son can really deny his mother?

I prayed hard and fast and concentrated on every word. If this plane was going down then I wanted to make sure I'd have some points earned to present at the pearly gates.

The plane started losing altitude and my thinking turned from prayer to one of trying to tabulate the chances of us surviving a crash landing. What if Joe was able to radio for help before we went down so that Coast Guard ships knew where to search? I've seen him fly and I'll bet he can slow this thing down just right so the crash really feels more like nothing but a rough landing. I'm pretty good at treading water and could probably do it for hours. Maybe something on this plane floated and we could hang onto it until help arrived. In the end, I think it was a combination of prayer and believing in Joe Hurston that allowed me to corral my fear and stuff it back down my throat.

Of course, he righted the plane and we made it to Baton Rouge on a single engine. It was right after landing that I started thinking nothing could ever happen to me if Joe Hurston was around. I don't know a lot about guardian angels but I know that I feel better, safer, when he's around.

Luckily for my buddy Wayne, he really had no idea what was going on during the flight. Of course, when we told him what happened his face took on an ashen tone. He later confessed to me that he doubted he could have kept his cool if the situation had gotten worse.

"I would have been toast," he said.

Somehow, with Joe Hurston aboard that plane, I doubt that very much.

We stayed in Baton Rouge for a night and ate some of the best gumbo I've ever tried. It was loaded with shrimp and crawfish and mussels and had that sneaky spice that gets you just right.

The next morning, I snuck into the Louisiana State University football stadium, which was housing thousands of refugees from New Orleans, except you weren't supposed to call them refugees. They were not letting media into the stadium but I just kind of wandered in and since I wasn't officially there on assignment, I figured I would do a few interviews and snap a few photos for a possible children's book. I actually parlayed the trip into two books, one for very young readers and one for fifth-graders.

The people staying at the LSU stadium were nice and willing to share their stories with me once they got over their distrust. I think I've been blessed with a disarming personality. I can often get people to talk to me and give me interviews when conventional wisdom told them not to. And I didn't feel as if I was exploiting these people, I was telling their story and letting their voices be heard. Any money I would make from the two very small books would be enough to cover expenses on the trip and a little more. I think people realize that I have a job to do and that I'm going to have to write a story with or without their cooperation. Wouldn't it be better for them to give their side of the story?

It's that disarming quality that would land me several interviews a few years later with a man whose son was brutally raped and murdered by a monster who was now on death row.

Without having yet seen New Orleans in person, it was hard for me to understand why so many of the people I interviewed had given up and were planning to relocate in the Houston area. Since most of their belongings were lost in the flooding, they really would have to start from scratch.

Some people told me about the dead bodies floating right down their streets, and others how they waited for days atop their roofs for helicopters to retrieve them. There was some sadness, a little resentment, and that collective huge melancholic sigh when you're faced with a monumental task.

There was also some anger, especially when the term "refugee" started getting thrown around.

I had invited myself into a private meeting where the national president of the NAACP was addressing some displaced people staying in the gymnasium at a Baton Rouge school. The American Red Cross was in charge and people were complaining about the facilities and how all the toilets were backing up and how sanitary conditions had degenerated quickly under the pressure of so many people.

I was probably the only non-African-American in the room. The NAACP leaders took turns urging the people not to give up as they spoke into a megaphone. They also weren't shy about riling the crowds up a bit too.

"I keep hearing the term refugee," one man bellowed. "Refugee? We are not refugees? We are not here from some other country seeking refuge. We are Americans, American citizens and we deserve the help that this country has to offer. Do not call us refugees."

If I have a talent for getting people to speak with me for articles or books I'm writing, then Joe has a knack for being able to talk himself and his water purifiers into just about any area he wants to go.

After seeing him operate in Indonesia, I had no doubt that he would be able to get us into the heart of New Orleans though the city was basically closed and under a sort of martial law. It wasn't all that safe as reports of armed gangs patrolling parts of the city were circulating and, of course, conditions in the city were still very much flooded.

We found the main NGO, or non-governmental organization, headquarters and Joe spent a few hours talking with whomever he needed to in order to secure a pair of passes that we could show at checkpoints around the city and grant us unfettered access.

Even as much of the massive flooding had receded, New Orleans was a sight. There were tall office buildings that had every single window blown in. There were old homes missing roofs or front doors. Water marks were high up on the side of buildings. Cars were flipped, piled into cul-de-sacs. But the most disconcerting thing about the city was that there was no one there. New Orleans was literally a ghost town. Sure there was the occasional straggler, the people who had refused to evacuate or those who felt conditions in the Superdome were too wretched for them to remain.

I met one couple who had gotten married only days before the storm hit and didn't really have enough money to leave town. They were OK until the windows of their apartment broke in and water started coming in from under the building's front door. They were lucky, they said, to be living on the second floor of the building. The water was waist-high on the ground-level apartments.

Their plan was to try and get work once the reconstruction of the city began and then save enough money to get to California. I guess one category 5 hurricane was enough for them.

We weren't sure how Joe's water purifiers would fare with some of the salinity issues in the city's streets so we brought cases of fresh water bottles with us anyway to hand out to whomever wanted them. There was really no one left in the city that could benefit from the purifiers anyway, meaning Joe would have to find an organization that could utilize them.

I remember one guy walking past us in the city. I held a bottle of water out to him and asked him if he would like some.

"Do I look thirsty to you?" he responded and walked away.

Back home, Jennifer was trying to adjust to life as a freelance writer. We had decided it would be better for her to stay at home with Isabelle at least for a few years and a great opportunity opened up for her as the featured correspondent in the dozen or so weekly newspapers that *Florida Today* produced.

She was assigned to cover the town we live in and some neighboring communities. It didn't involve any heavy stories as much of what she covered was pretty light and community-oriented.

I know it was tough for her to stay home while I seemed to be jetting all over the world writing interesting stories. She's a heck of a writer and sometimes felt underappreciated. But I truly appreciate her making that sacrifice to give up her career as a staff writer in order to make sure Isabelle was raised right.

We had a lot of help with Isabelle too, which was nice.

Jennifer's mother and stepfather lived only 20 minutes from us and could be counted on to help babysit once in a while even on some overnight stints when we needed a break. And my parents, who do a great job playing grandparents to all five kids, lived three hours away in Hudson Beach on the west coast of Florida.

My dad had taken a part-time job driving a school bus for troubled kids who were court-ordered to attend a Maritime Institute nearby. Mom spent her days gardening, bowling, and socializing with friends. Once Isabelle was born, my mom really wanted to be part of it. So, while Isabelle was still too young for school, mom took her for a week every two months.

They took her to the zoo and to amusement parks and the movies and swimming. And every time I picked Isabelle up from them, she was wearing a new outfit with new shoes and new toys.

As they got older, I think my parents felt it was important that they developed a strong relationship with Isabelle, whom I refer to as the baby, even to this day.

Jennifer was doing so well for a while that she was actually making more money as a freelancer than she was as a staff writer at the paper. For a few years we enjoyed nice prosperity as she could barely keep up with the massive amount of work that was being thrown her way. Of course, once the recession started creeping in, the first place *Florida Today* started making cutbacks in was in their freelance budget.

During that time, I was assigned another yearlong project, but this time I could leave my passport home. I was asked to follow two hospice care nurses and the patients they were seeing. So, after making all the arrangements—remember how disarming I could be?—I spent every Tuesday for eight months with a pair of nurses and their wonderful dying patients.

I was amazed at how these two women—Diane and Judy—could minister and care for dying people every single day. I mean, they were nurses, and nurses are trained to help people get better. But these nurses were charged with helping people get ready to die, people whose life had run out of options. It was pretty somber stuff and yet they were the funniest pair of characters I think I've ever covered.

They filled the homes of the dying with sunshine and jokes and laughter and concern. They gave so much of themselves that you wondered how long they could continue before they ran out of love and compassion. Mitch Albom had "Tuesday's with Morrie," and I had "Tuesdays with Judy and Diane."

These two women also went way above the call of duty for their patients. I witnessed them feeding their pets, making phone calls for them, cleaning their kitchens, and listening to their fears.

I remember one of the patients in particular. She was a little old woman who lived all alone in a mobile home park in the city of Palm Bay. Margaret was tiny, thin, and fragile and she was suffering from just about every ailment you could think of. There was nothing else really that doctors or a hospital could do for her so they sent her home and she was checked on by nurses several times a week.

She always greeted me with a hug and a kiss on my cheek and would sit me down at her kitchen table and tell me stories of her youth. Without fail, however, the stories of picnics and first dates and World War II would ultimately lead to her son who died of an overdose years earlier. She would show me photos and talk about how handsome he was and how very much she missed him.

She would always end up crying.

"I wish I could kill myself," she would say. "I am so tired and in so much pain all the time that I wish I could just die already. I would kill myself but I know my son is waiting for me in heaven. They wouldn't let me into heaven if I ever did anything as terrible as killing myself."

I just listened with a sympathetic ear.

One week she surprised me with a new outfit she had purchased for my daughter Isabelle. I could not believe the generosity of this woman's spirit. Here she was suffering and waiting to die while dealing with the emotional torture of having had buried her own son, yet she had time to think about me. I learned that she had given money to a friend to get the outfit for Isabelle.

Before she died, I repaid her kindness by bringing Isabelle with me on my weekly visit. Margaret's face lit up like I had never seen. She simply could not believe that I had brought my little girl with me to meet her. She lay on the bed next to Isabelle and doted on her, kissing her and hugging her. She cried again, but this time they were tears of joy.

That entire experience and the wonderful people I met taught me so much about the power of the human spirit and how happiness and peace is all people really crave.

I will never forget any of them, especially Margaret.

The newspaper published a 28-page special section, entitled "Guardians on Life's Final Journey," of my experiences with hospice and it won several statewide journalism awards. But a few months later my executive editor asked me if I was going to be in the office the following day because there was a phone call he wanted me to take.

The next day I sat fidgety in his office, nervous but excited because I knew it had to be something good, awaiting the call. Finally, one of the head honchos for Gannett called and congratulated me for winning the Outstanding Achievement in Writing Award for the company. Of all 80-plus newspapers and thousands of reporters, I was the one chosen! It was quite an honor made doubly nice by the $5,000 check that accompanied it. Of course, $5,000 was just about what I owed my divorce attorney so it was another case of easy-come, easy-go.

The award had another little unofficial bonus. Gannet asked me if I would be interested in being part of the comprehensive coverage in the upcoming winter Olympic Games in Torino. I was flabbergasted.

The plan would be for me to spend close to five weeks in Italy covering all the sledding sports: bobsled, skeleton, and luge.

Of course, that is, if my wife was OK with being on her own for all that time. I was a little nervous asking her if it would be all right, but as usual she told me that I needed to jump at such a rare and special opportunity. How many people, she argued, get a chance to cover the Olympics! She was right, of course, and it would also be great for my career.

I sure was happy that Joe Hurston had urged me to drive to Miami and get my passport even before I had met him in person.

I spent the weeks leading up to the Olympics learning all I could about sledding sports and even rented out the movie *Cool Runnings* about the improbable Jamaican bobsled team to watch with the family. It turned out we even had a local angle for my newspaper, *Florida Today*. The track coach for one of the local high schools had actually once been an alternate for the U.S. bobsled team in the Olympics. Peter Blount was recruited, as were other college track stars during that time, to come and try out for the squad.

He shared with me a wealth of information and some great stories about the sport.

I was ready for the sledding sports. But I wasn't ready for the cold and the altitude. Holy moly was it cold there. I shouldn't complain too much. I basically had two apartments to myself—one in the city of Turin or Torino and one in the Italian Alps. I was also given temporary use of a laptop, blackberry, special cell phone, and all types of other cool gadgets.

Before the sledding sports began, I spent most of my time in Torino, covering press conferences with people like Shawn White or the American female hockey team or flamboyant figure skater Johnny Weir. It was great fun meeting all these world-class athletes and then eating some of the best food in the world at night.

There wasn't a whole lot of free time, which was OK with me because I was kind of lonely. Besides obviously missing Jennifer and the kids, I also didn't really know a lot of the others who were part of the coverage team.

But when I did have a day off, I tried to take advantage of what Italy had to offer. One day I went to a Juventus soccer game and was blown away by the riot police, the chanting, the drum-playing, and the flag-waving. It was an incredible experience, even though it was pretty darned cold.

The next time I had a few hours to myself I decided to take a cab to downtown Torino and find the Shroud of Turin. Without much trouble, I found the Cathedral of St. John the Baptist, the large Catholic church which houses the shroud. Now, for those of you who don't know, the shroud is a burial cloth that bears an image on it of a man who suffered wounds very similar to what Jesus suffered when He was put to death on the cross.

I knew there exists a lot of controversy about whether the shroud is the true burial cloth of Jesus. No one has been quite able to figure out what caused the image to appear. Believers say it was from the energy that God expended in raising His son from the dead. But others say it is not real and that the material was made 1,000 years after Christ died.

In any event, I went to go check it out. I was disappointed to learn that the shroud itself is put on display only once every 10 years or so and was locked safely away. However, near the rear of the old church there is a display with an exact replica of the shroud. I wandered back slowly and was suddenly moved to tears the instant the shroud came into view.

It was unfolded carefully above what appeared to be a white marble container or even coffin that I thought might house the original. The display was very simple with the only other item displayed behind the glass being a crown of thorns.

I knew it wasn't even the real shroud and I knew all about the doubt surrounding the real shroud, yet in that moment I believed with all my heart that that piece of cloth once covered the body of Jesus shortly after He was crucified. Don't ask me how I knew, it was just one of those "a-ha!" moments in life.

I sat there for probably an hour quietly looking at the shroud and when I looked at the crown of thorns I could do nothing but weep. I couldn't really explain what happened to me that day at the back of this cathedral, except to say that my heart had never felt so much pity. But looking back, maybe I was crying because I missed Jesus so much. I needed Him, I missed Him, I just couldn't admit it to myself. And so much time had passed between visits with Him that I just didn't feel worthy. Maybe I cried because I put that wound in his side, or through his hands and feet. Maybe it was my sins that continued to place the crown of thorns over his head.

Whatever the reason, I found myself going back and sitting with the shroud every chance I could.

EIGHT

YOU WOULD THINK that by now, after all I had seen, I would have somehow found a way to accept God's invitation and get Him back into my life. But some of us are more stubborn than others, and so despite admiring and even loving Joe Hurston and what he stood for, despite my experience with the Shroud of Turin or the giving nurses or dying patients, I was still afraid or reluctant to let God in.

But the thing about God is He never gives up.

Now, on the home front, things between Jennifer and myself were good as we worked together to raise our children. It wasn't always easy as our ex-spouses seemed to be jealous of our happiness and would do petty things to try and annoy us. Most of the time we just ignored them and went on living our dream lives together.

Looking back, though, there was something missing from our relationship besides God. Jennifer's biological father was Jewish and her mother was a lapsed Catholic who had become an atheist. So, she never really grew up with any sort of spiritual teaching or guidance. How can you miss what you've never known, right? Looking back, we didn't have a lot of real good close friends. We got invited to the parties and to the beach and stuff but I mean real friends, like the kind you can really rely on.

Just about the only friend I had was Joe Hurston, who lived about an hour away and who spent most of his time globetrotting around the world with his water purifiers and tending to his ink cartridge company.

It was the fact that he was expanding his company and moving into a new building that prompted Jennifer and me to attend his grand opening party. It was actually a pretty nice affair with hundreds of people in attendance. Now Joe was a guy who had friends.

There was a slide show presentation about his company and how he really only works to fund his missionary work and the water purifiers. I was mentioned a few times and it was kind of nice that some of the people there actually knew who I was as he had spoken of me to them.

After the meal, Jennifer and I were mingling, though it was difficult with Isabelle wanting to run around and touch absolutely everything. Just before we were getting ready to call it a night and head back home, Joe grabbed me by the elbow and dragged me over to meet someone that he had wanted to introduce me to for a long time.

Now, while I do consider myself a friendly person that is easy to talk to, I'm not crazy about forced introductions followed by awkward small talk and an even more uncomfortable goodbye. And while I love Joe dearly, I was internally cringing as we neared this bent-backed older man with the heavy slow drawl.

He introduced the man as Robert Bland. Bland? How can someone go through life with the name Bland? Also, this guy looked as about as exciting to talk with as his last name indicated. Still, I was already there and would just have to get it over with.

As he started talking to me, many people were saying goodbye, patting me on the shoulder and I could see Jennifer chasing Isabelle through the maze of people. It would only be a matter of time before Isabelle would implode into a crying fit. It really was time to go and I didn't want to spend an hour in the car with a cranky toddler and an even crankier wife.

Maybe he could tell that I was only half-listening because he kept putting his hand on my arm as if to say "listen to this, you really need to hear it."

He told me that he ran an organization that was sort of like a boot camp for teenagers interested in becoming missionaries. It was on nearby Merritt Island and every summer, kids from all over the country came and trained there before going off on a real mission trip.

By this time I was slightly interested, thinking that it might make for a nice feature story once the camp got under way.

"But this year," he continued, "we've got a new program started up. It's part of what we call our Orphan Angels program. We're gonna send groups of kids, American teenagers, with little more than the clothes on their backs, to Zambia, Africa. These kids won't be allowed to take suitcases or electronics or anything like that. We need them to travel light so that we can give them each a 70-pound bag of shoes and socks. These teams, we call them foot-washing teams, are going to go and wash the feet of AIDS orphans and then put a clean pair of socks and shoes on them."

As he spoke, his old blue eyes twinkled a bit and there was real life to them. His face was kind and he measured his words carefully.

"AIDS is still a terrible epidemic over there and these kids, well, many of them are sick with AIDS and others have no one at all to take care of them because their parents died of AIDS. If they're lucky enough to stay with a family then they sleep out with the animals, get no blanket, eat only after everyone else has been fed, and they never get to go to school. Like Jesus washed the feet of his apostles, these teenagers will wash the feet of these orphans."

I stood there silently, not able to speak because of the tears that were leaking out of the corner of my eyes.

"This," I finally was able to muster, "is something that I have to see."

I was moved by the story of humility and service. These American teenagers are going to be living and breathing the Gospel. They are really going to travel halfway across the globe to wash the feet of total strangers, children who might even be sick with AIDS. The more I thought about it, the more I wanted to go.

I must have driven Jennifer crazy the entire ride home talking about wanting to go to Africa and about all the Hemingway stories I had read over the years that take place in Africa. I know that in her sweet heart and mind she wished she could have just said "yes, of course you should go." But I also knew the reality of the worsening economy and the fact that the number of available freelance assignments had dropped drastically cutting her pay. Like it or not, we had to admit that our finances were suffering. She was very diplomatic and told me I should pitch the idea at the newspaper first and see what they say. I know it probably killed her to see me so anxious to go and her knowing that I probably would not be able to.

Still, I held on to some hope. After all, the trip was still several months away and maybe I could somehow swing the money myself.

All weekend long I plotted and planned exactly how I would pitch the story to my editors. Of course, I knew the answer would be "no." Newspapers typically don't write about Christians or Christian ideals. They just don't. Even if a newspaper is serving a community that is 95 percent Christian and 95 percent pro-life, chances are the editorial board will be pro-choice. It's that double standard that permeates society. When artists, writers, and filmmakers depict Jesus as being gay, or the offspring of rape it is looked on as art. But would any of those writers, artists, or filmmakers have the guts to do similar stories on Muslim tenets or the Jewish faith the way they approach Christians? Probably not. Do you know why? Because Muslims and Jews would never stand for it.

Anyway, I knew that my newspaper was not very Christian, and to be quite honest that was all right with me because I wasn't very Christian either. Seriously, who would care about a group of teenaged Christian missionaries doing good deeds? But I really, really wanted to get to Africa.

I knew that first-thing Monday morning would not be a good thing since the editors would be too busy going through the weekend's e-mails and putting out any fires. Right before the 10:30 meeting is also no good because the editors are busy organizing the stories they plan to pitch or the ones they want to save for later in the week.

So I waited until a little bit after the 10:30 meeting leaving myself with a little bit of a window before lunch.

I went into my editor's office and started my well-rehearsed spiel. I tried not to sound too excited—they react better to things when they think it's their idea. I downplayed the whole Christian angle and focused on the service, the shoes, and the fact that they also help plant gardens, do medical clinics, and other things. I also downplayed the cost, since I learned that everyone would be sleeping in tents.

I tried to make it sound—as best as I could—that I would be sacrificing comfort and safety and time from my family in order to get the paper a great story. When I was done making my pitch, I was quite satisfied that I had given it my best shot. Now, Plan B would have involved trying to save money over the next few months to be able to go on my own dime.

But to my shock and internal joy, the editor did not laugh, scoff, or shoot the idea down. In fact, he said it would be a great story and he'd like to take the idea further up the chain. But there was one thing missing before he could do that. He instructed me to find out if any local teens were making the trip.

Buoyed by his enthusiasm I found out all the information needed, cost, dates, storylines, and yes, a 17-year-old girl from Satellite Beach was making the trip.

I was going to Africa.

I needed to make sure my vaccinations were in order and that I had a prescription for anti-malarial tablets. I made an appointment with Dr. Steve Badolato. Now, I had not gone to him in a while because, well he didn't really want to treat me after I had written a series of articles basically blaming insurance companies and not attorneys for the rising medical malpractice insurance premiums.

I was hoping he would not remember that he practically told me to find another doctor. But he seemed happy to see me when I arrived and he spent a great deal of time with me researching the health hazards I could potentially face in Africa.

When the visit was over, he told me to come back and see him for a follow-up appointment when I returned. He also said he admired what I was doing and waived my co-pay.

My dad was very nervous about me going to Africa and he gave me a small wooden cross to keep with me at all times. And even though Jennifer and I were not practicing Christians, she too bought me a silver cross and chain that she wanted me to wear around my neck.

Now, I have to admit that my trip to Mumbai sullied any expectations I had of Zambia, Africa. Part of me was dying to get there and see the things my longtime idol, Ernest Hemingway, had seen. But part of me expected it to be dirty, polluted, crowded, and unpleasant. I was a little nervous.

But after stopping in London—where I explored Piccadilly Circus—then Johannesburg, South Africa, my photographer and I finally landed in the small airport in Ndola, Zambia. And I knew the second I stepped off the plane that I was going to love this trip. There were thatched roof huts, swaying palm trees, tall elephant grass. The ground was red, hardened clay and the people had dark, shiny faces with big beautiful smiles.

Doug and Barb Petersen were there to greet us. They were the team leaders for the "Foot washing team," and lived in Zambia 10 months a year. They were grandparents from the Midwest who had given up everything, even seeing their own families at Christmas, in order to serve the Lord, here in Zambia.

I liked them instantly: Barb with her snowy-white hair, whose outer appearance gave absolutely no indication of how tough she was. I remember how one morning she was driving us and we came upon one of dozens of checkpoints on the major roads. These were manned by young soldiers or policemen who would seek bribes in order to let you pass. Bribery like that is very much part of the culture in many third-world countries.

"What do you have for me today Miss?" the soldier asked, holding out his hand.

"Today I have a smile and a heartfelt 'good morning,'" Barb answered. The soldier started laughing straight from his belly and said something to his compatriot.

"Good morning to you too," he replied and waved us on.

Barb explained that once you set a precedent and start paying, you'll never be able to pass without giving a bribe. She did admit to giving them cold bottles of soda sometimes, when Doug wasn't around.

If Ernest Hemingway had been an evangelical missionary, instead of a writer, he would have been Doug Petersen. I was totally impressed by Doug, a barrel-chested man, who had spent the last 20 years of his life building villages throughout Africa and leading teenagers through unforgettable experiences.

He didn't drink or smoke and had a little bit of a pot-belly. His blue eyes were so light that they were almost gray when he squinted. His one weakness was chicken and coca-cola, which he would have eaten for every meal if Barb had let him.

Doug and Barb were the most genuine people I ever met and I loved them by the time my trip was over.

When we arrived at the base camp, I sat outside with Doug for a bit as the sun started to set. I couldn't believe my good fortune, having made it to Africa. The dying sun was turning the sky orange and the women working in the base's banana plantation were singing African songs. It was a moment straight from a movie.

I asked Doug if he had ever run into trouble and he smiled and gave me a look with eyes that said, "Well, you know, we have been here for a very long time."

The reporter in me pressed him for more details and he counted the number of times they had been robbed or that someone had tried to rob them. Luckily, they never had been present during any of the political violence and upheaval that Africa is sometimes known for, although violence found them one time.

It happened in neighboring Zimbabwe. Doug and Barb were living there doing some missionary work and their house was probably the nicest in the area. One night two men broke in and were rummaging through the place when Doug saw them and frightened them off.

A few months later, the rains had come and Doug—in addition to chicken and coca-cola —loved storms. He sat out on the porch and watched the rain move closer from miles and miles away. Then the lightning started to flash and light up the sky. There was just something in the power of storms that Doug loved. But when he started hearing his wife, Barb, speak in slow, hushed tones from inside the house, he knew something was wrong. He headed inside and almost instantly walked right into the two men that had tried to rob the house previously. This time they had a gun and before Doug could even say a word, two shots rang out.

A slug passed through his right arm and another right through the chest. He crumpled to the ground instantly and found himself sitting in an ever-growing pool of blood. Barb ran to the bathroom where she kept a stun gun because she heard it helps neutralize the venom in snake bites.

"Madam has a gun," one of the assailants cried and they fled.

Barb called for one of their assistants and they got Doug into the truck.

His breathing was already shallow and they could not find a way to stop the bleeding. The rains had washed out many of the roads and the trip to the hospital would take hours. The situation was getting darker by the moment and Barb held her dying husband in her arms.

By this time, I was completely mesmerized.

"So what did you do? I mean, what were you thinking at that moment?"

"Well to be honest, I didn't think I was going to make it. I could barely speak and I knew that I had only a certain number of breaths left," he said before smiling sadly and fidgeting as if remembering caused the wound to flare up. "So I knew exactly how I wanted to use those last few breaths. I wanted to praise God and then thank Him. I just started thanking Him."

"Thanking Him?" I couldn't believe it. Why on earth would anyone thank God right after getting shot? Me? I would have been cursing all the way up to high heaven. But not Doug, he decided to spend his last seconds alive praising God.

"Doug, I'm not quite sure I understand. Why were you thanking Him?"

"I was thanking Him for always being so faithful."

Still, I did not understand but said nothing. Perhaps he could sense my confusion and continued.

"All my life, Jesus stood by me and came through with every single thing that was promised me in the gospels. All of it is true and He was always faithful to me."

I was speechless. Yet at the same time I was beginning to understand.

"I never felt His presence more than at that time," he said, as he unbuttoned his shirt to show this "doubting Thomas" the scar from where the bullet entered his body.

One of the men was quickly captured and was sentenced to ten years in prison. But before he was to start serving his sentence, Doug was able to convince the magistrate to allow the man to visit the Petersens at home. There, Doug shared dinner and the Gospel with the man.

By the time they were done with supper, the man was weeping. He begged Doug to forgive him.

He didn't have to. They remain friends to this day.

The Zambian police urged the Petersens to invest in a real gun for protection. But even though Doug was nearly shot to death, a firearm is something they would never consider.

"How would it look if missionaries went around shooting people?" Barb asked. "Isn't it better for us to get shot and go to heaven?"

The next few days were magical. There is no other way really to describe them. We traveled with the foot washing team on the back of trucks or on motorcycles, passing open copper mines, little villages and through cities. It was hot, we were hungry, and the red clay made our clothes dusty but no one complained.

We were all just so thankful to be there. I had never met such positive and loving people as those teenagers. I guess I was expecting them to be a little creepy or very over-the-top evangelical. But they weren't. They were just filled with love.

I knew their attitude was rubbing off on me when I caught myself humming "God of Wonders," and even learning a few of the lines to sing in my head.

"God of wonders beyond our galaxy, you are holy, the universe declares your majesty, you are holy. Lord of heaven and earth."

The song was an earworm that had burrowed into my head and now I couldn't get rid of it.

I think the first village we pulled into was Kitwe and the children came running behind our truck waving to us the entire way. They had heard we were coming and so the schoolmaster declared a holiday. After all, it's not every day that you receive your first pair of shoes.

I wanted to be there to witness and videotape the very first child whose feet were being washed. Several different lines were set up and I knelt down next to a girl from Washington State who told me that she did all types of fundraisers from pancake breakfasts to spaghetti dinners in her backyard to be able to afford the trip.

The team leaders told the teenagers that they should wear rubber gloves because some of these children had AIDS and things could get dicey if there were any open wounds. But this girl from Washington, I think her name was Ann, looked at me and threw the rubber gloves aside.

"Would you want someone to wear rubber gloves when they washed your feet?" she asked me. "I know I wouldn't."

Her toughness evaporated in a moment, however, when the first child approached. She was wearing her dusty school uniform. Even though the children were on holiday it was likely the only clothing she had.

Her big brown eyes were slightly lighter than the color of her skin. Her face looked as if it had been a very long time since she last used it to laugh or smile. She looked way too serious for a 10-year-old.

And in a moment I felt as if I knew this girl. I felt that I knew her pain and her suffering. I knew just by looking at her that her father contracted AIDS from a prostitute while away working the copper mines and that he had infected her mother. I knew they were dead. I knew this little girl was forced to look after her siblings and somehow fend for herself. I knew that the school uniform had been donated because it was too large for her.

I know that she had never watched an episode of "SpongeBob SquarePants" and that she had never been to a zoo or an aquarium or an amusement park. I knew she had never ridden on a carousel and had never been to a movie theater.

But looking at her, approaching slowly and shyly, I knew in my heart of hearts that God was holding her hand. There could be no other explanation for her survival.

Ann from Washington must have known this as well because the second that little girl placed her dried, cracking dusty feet into the basin of water, she started to cry.

And seeing Ann cry made me cry as well.

"I'm just so humbled and so thankful to be washing this little girl's feet," she sobbed quietly.

"Why are you crying?" I asked.

"Because this is the first time in my life that I know for a fact that I am doing what Jesus wants me to do."

She put the shoes and socks on the little girl with sad eyes and there it was, a smile. And I knew that for the first time in my life I was where I was supposed to be as well.

The African children were wonderful. They were beautiful and friendly and wanted nothing from you but your attention, your company.

A visiting priest gave a great sermon at our church recently about Eucharistic adoration and spending time in the chapel. He talked about his two big old St. Bernard dogs and how he traveled with them everywhere from church to church. In fact, he had them waiting just outside our church resting in the shade of a palm tree.

He said that he had awakened in the middle of the night to use the restrooms and being in an unfamiliar rectory, stumbled over one of his sleeping dogs and twisted his knee. As he was icing his knee in the morning before mass, someone asked him why he goes through the trouble of packing them up and their gigantic cages and schlepping them wherever he goes.

"My dogs," he told the congregation, "want only one thing. They just want to be with me."

That's what those little children wanted. They just wanted to be with me.

Every morning I would see them with the paper plates I had discarded the night before or the plastic spoons I had tossed in the trash. One little boy found my empty soda bottle and I swear every time I saw him that week he was clutching it.

My photographer, Craig, whose photo of me adorns the cover of this book, was taking pictures of me posing with the children one day. If there is anything these kids loved it was posing for photos.

But this particular instance, after snapping one after another, we were off to go do our reporting when a little boy kept tugging at my hand and trying to say something in English. I knelt down and listened as closely as I could. It took me a while to understand what he was saying but I finally deciphered his message.

"One boy. One boy," he kept saying.

Still I didn't know what he meant.

He put his arms up for me to pick him up and he was nothing more than skin and bones. He pointed at Craig and repeated his plea.

"One boy, one boy," he said and it hit me. All he wanted was to be the only boy in the photograph with me.

That photograph, of little Franco in my arms, hangs proudly on a wall in my home.

The next day was when I knelt down to videotape an 88-year-old man who had wandered into camp and saw Jesus Christ.

I told no one of my experience until I returned home two days later to my lovely wife. She said that we need to go to church that Sunday.

Holy Name of Jesus Catholic Church is a beautiful and majestic place. It is directly across the street from the ocean and less than two miles from my home. But from the minute I stepped into the church that day I noticed how much love there was. I still wasn't sure I belonged there, having only been an Easter and Christmas churchgoer, but I figured I should give it a try after what had happened.

That day happened to be August 6 the day when Catholics celebrate the feast day of the Transfiguration of Jesus. This holiday commemorates when Jesus allowed some of his apostles to see Him in His true glory, allowing them to recognize Him as the son of God.

Our pastor, Father David Page, a small, very kind and elderly Irish priest who was nearing 50 years of service to God, gave the sermon. And it was during that homily that his words reached down and touched my heart.

"There are times in life when Jesus," he said, "will allow you to see Him. Sometimes it may be when a child is born or in the passing of a loved one but sometimes He will show himself to you."

I turned instantly to Jennifer who was staring right back at me with a huge grin on her face.

During the closing hymn, I turned to her and said, "We're coming back next week."

We did and that Sunday there was a priest visiting from Africa. He gave a wonderful sermon and like Ann from Washington, I finally knew I was where Jesus wanted me. In fact, I remember laughing after mass that God must really want me here at church.

He never gave up and He never gave up searching for me. No matter how many times I had thrown Him to the side, He kept coming back.

There were men and women standing outside of church that Sunday wearing the same shirts with a stitched-on emblem that read "Christ Renews His Parish."

They were trying to get people to come sign up for men's and women's weekend retreats held on separate weekends. They were quite persistent and so I signed up not fully committed in my heart to going. Jennifer did as well.

We sort of forgot about the retreat, which was being held over the first two weekends of September and went on with our lives. Things were different, better, as we started to look at the world and the daily struggles of life just a little differently.

Things even seemed different at the newspaper. While I was writing my series of articles about the Christian teenagers in Africa, the editors told me to play up the Christian angle. What? We never write about Christian issues and faith, even though our county is more than 90 percent Christian.

I did, of course, and what followed were four days of stories and videos for our website that were very well received by our readers. I received dozens of e-mails and letters thanking me for writing about faith and God in the real world.

Even my doctor, Steve Badolato, had read every word of the series. When I went to go see him for my follow-up visit, he praised the stories over and over. He said he had never read anything like that in the newspaper.

Then he said if I ever needed a doctor along on one of my trips that he would be glad to come with me. I took those words and locked them in my vault.

The weekend of Jennifer's retreat arrived and she was torn. We had received an invitation from her father to visit him in West Palm Beach and she didn't know what to do. Ultimately, perhaps thanks to my pressure, she agreed to go on the retreat.

I was worried sick all weekend for her. I was picturing her surrounded by a bunch of Jesus freaks preaching to her. Maybe this had been a big mistake, yes, we were back in the fold but were we really ready for something like this? A weekend committed to this kind of activity was probably pushing it for people like us. I even had nightmares about it.

On Sunday evening I waited anxiously for her to return. I was hoping she would not be angry with me for forcing her to go.

There was a definite glow about her when she came up the walkway. She was smiling.

"It was the best weekend of my life," she said, and I could feel my heart leaping for joy.

The next weekend was my turn and she was right. It was an incredible weekend of friendship and fellowship, of listening to testimony and stories of conversion. The greatest thing was that these men were exactly like me. They had fallen, they had sinned, they too felt they had been unworthy of God's love. Yet, here they were because God did not give up on them either.

While I won't give away the "secret" surprises of that magical weekend, one highlight I will share were the letters received during the weekend. There were letters of support from friends, relatives, and even strangers.

I cried reading them, surprised by the number of people who cared about me.

One letter struck me more than the rest. It was from someone I had never met, someone involved in the retreat process.

"Dear John, you did not know this, but I have been praying for you for the last six months," the letter began. It went on to say how important I was to God and how He would do anything for me.

It closed with a quote from the Old Testament. It was Isaiah 49:15.

"See! I have not forgotten you. I have carved you in the palm of my hands."

NINE

JENNIFER AND I and the children became regular churchgoers. We made friends and even became part of the Christ Renews His Parish formation teams. Suddenly we wondered how was it that we had gone all those years without the love, hope, and comfort that Jesus brings.

With this new infusion of faith and God in my life, I was introduced to the terrible story of Junny Rios-Martinez. Let me back up a bit. In the newspaper business, you tend to run into a lot of negative people. I receive e-mails and anonymous phone calls daily, telling me what a terrible job I did on a story or complaining about this or that. For some reason, many out there in the general public do not perceive journalists to be actual human beings. Maybe they group us in with lawyers or IRS accountants. I don't know.

I used to let the malcontents get to me and sometimes I would find myself in an e-mail confrontation or tug of war trying to prove or explain why I wrote a certain story. It drove me crazy that I was never able to get them to see my point of view. But my newly rediscovered Catholic faith gave me the strength to be direct and honest and kind instead of mean-spirited. I thanked them for taking the time to express their view, asked them to consider mine, and urged them to continue reading the newspaper.

Of course, that did not work with everyone, and with people who were abusive or who insisted on limiting their vocabulary to foul language I simply asked them to never e-mail me again. Life is too short to get into these no-win situations and arguments with people who let negativity rule their thinking.

I began to try and let my Christianity come through in my reporting and writing and in how I simply carried myself at work. Sometimes it meant showing more compassion and many times it simply forced me to be more patient with people—like editors—than I would have been in the past.

But my faith would never help me through a story as much as it did in the Junny Rios Martinez case.

Junny was an 11-year-old boy who had been raped and killed in Brevard County many years before I even arrived at *Florida Today*. I had heard the name and how there was some connection to the newspaper but never really dug deeper. Reading and reporting about abused and murdered children is something I try and avoid when I can.

But in early 2007, I learned that the young boy's killer, Mark Dean Schwab, was running out of appeals and would likely be the next inmate in Florida to be executed by the use of lethal injection. It was time to write some stories and learn a little more about the case.

Schwab had already been a convicted child rapist who only served three years of an eight-year sentence by the time he was released from prison in 1981. The tall, skinny, bespectacled man was only in his early 20s and had plenty of time to turn his life around. But his appetite for hurting young boys was apparently insatiable.

Looking through a copy of *Florida Today* one afternoon, Schwab saw a photo taken at a kite festival at a local school. The photo showed a sweet-faced boy with short blonde hair flying his kite.

Schwab became obsessed and started initiating contact with the family. Knowing the parents were not at the school and did not meet the *Florida Today* photographer who snapped the photo, he called the house impersonating the photographer.

He said Junny would be perfect for a photo essay and wanted to shoot more photos. First he needed to learn a little bit more about the boy and subsequently learned that he played Little League baseball and was an aspiring surfer.

A few days went by and Schwab went to the family's Cocoa home in a subdivision of well-maintained homes with big backyards and manicured lawns. He made up a fake *Florida Today* badge and said he was friends with the photographer who shot the kite photos. He tried to befriend the family, though they were leery of the enthusiasm he had for their son.

Schwab learned that Junny wanted to be a professional surfer more than anything and promised that he would help in any way he could. He claimed to have contacts at surfing magazines and that he was sure with the right story in a surfing publication that he could land the youngster a corporate sponsor.

Days went by and there were more phone calls from Schwab who was now known to the family as Mark Dean. This was in the days before sex offenders had to register with police and their actions and movements were scrutinized more closely. He seemed to have the right credentials and they had no reason to doubt him or his motives. Schwab provided the family with fake contracts from a fictitious company that had agreed to sponsor the child's surfing endeavors. He had a T-shirt made up bearing the company's logo that he gave the boy.

He even told the boy that he could design his own surfboard and that it would be delivered soon.

Finally, the predator had enough stalking and wanted more. He set up a photo shoot at a studio in Daytona Beach where he could introduce Junny to his new surfing sponsors. The plan was for the young boy and Schwab to go alone. But Junny's parents were not very comfortable with that and at the last minute they decided to go along as well.

Schwab was forced to cancel the shoot.

He would have to resort to plan B. It would not be difficult. He already knew so much about the boy and his habits that any number of plans would have likely worked.

On April 18, 1991, Schwab called Junny's elementary school and pretended to be the boy's father. He told the secretary that he wanted to practice baseball with Junny before that night's big game and so he should not get on the bus but walk to the baseball field instead.

Junny said goodbye to a friend he was walking with, hopped the fence at the ball-field, and was surprised to see his "friend" Mark Dean Schwab.

Schwab told the boy that he had cleared it with his parents to take him to see his new surfboard. No one ever saw Junny alive again.

The monster took the boy to a Cocoa Beach hotel, amid dozens of surfing stores. He beat the boy. He raped him. He killed him.

Schwab then put the boy's body into a footlocker, dumped it in a rural part of the county, and left town.

When Junny was a no-show for his 6:30 p.m. baseball game that night, the family knew that Schwab had something to do with it. A manhunt was on. Eventually, Schwab was apprehended in Ohio and brought back to Brevard County. He told police that someone forced him to rape and kill the child.

He led police to the badly decomposed body.

Learning this, all of this, made me sick. Mark Dean Schwab was a predator in the truest sense. He was indeed a monster and at that moment, I hated him. I was glad that his execution was pending and I was hoping that he was afraid.

Over the next few months I did a series of stories about the case and the wrangling in the state capital of Tallahassee over when the governor would sign Schwab's death warrant. But when it came down to meeting the family, I have to admit that I was extremely nervous. What could I possibly say to them that would give them comfort? I would be doing nothing but stirring up 15-year-old wounds.

With trepidation and a heavy-heart for what they must have suffered, I drove to the same house they still lived in, the house where their precious boy would lay his head every night. I drove past the small playground and park that bears their son's name and a chill went through me.

The boy's father, Junny Sr., is thin and not very tall at all. He has wild, staring eyes, a receding hairline and is tenacious as a pit bull. He is a tremendous jazz and salsa percussionist who still plays occasionally in the county.

His wife, Vickie, is the polar opposite. She is blonde, quiet, private and chooses her words very carefully.

They welcomed me into their home where incense was burning and smooth jazz was playing softly in the background.

"Torres, huh? Puerto Rican? I'm Puerto Rican too. I did some checking on you," he smiled. "People told me that you're the best they have over there at the newspaper. I'm glad because I only want the best working on this story."

When he asked me if I had children, I learned that the interview would have been over if my answer had been no.

"People who don't have children think they understand, they think they know," he said. "But no one can know that kind of love until you have children yourself. You know what I mean? Only you can know what it would do to you if some sick pervert, some monster did that to one of your children."

We sat down and talked and we instantly hit it off. Clearly, this man had a gigantic heart but he would never ever recover from having it broken so severely 15 years earlier. He was eager to show me his son's trophies, his photographs, his Little League videos, and his surfboards. Junny's presence was everywhere. I could feel it like a cloud of sadness over this family.

Our getting-along made me bold enough to ask Junny about a rumor I had long heard that he snuck a gun into the courthouse and was prepared to kill the man who murdered his son. He stood up and smiled. It was almost as if he was thinking, "Finally, someone has the nerve to actually ask me."

He described how the security guards at the courthouse knew him and his family and would not force them to go through the metal detector if they were running late. Knowing this, Junny bought a handgun, made sure he was late, and carried it into the courtroom without a second look.

"The plan was simple," he said. "I was going to stand up, pull the gun out, and go blam, blam blam, then drop the gun and hold my hands straight up in the air. I was waiting and waiting for the exact moment."

Sensing his agitation or nervousness, his wife Vickie urged him not to do whatever it was he was planning.

A second time, Junny told me, he had purchased a high powered hunting rifle with a scope that would allow him to hit a target from a few hundred yards away. He stationed himself on a hill that overlooked the area where deputies unloaded prisoners going to trial at the courthouse.

He sat there waiting for Schwab to arrive. He held up the gun and put the child-killer in his sights. But he would not have been able to fire without possibly injuring a deputy. And that, he said, was unacceptable.

During this time period, I decided to ramp up my involvement in the church by volunteering to help with perpetual adoration. For those who are unfamiliar, perpetual adoration is a tiny chapel at the church where the consecrated host, the Eucharist, the body of Christ is kept.

For Catholics, it is a very sacred place and we believe that Jesus is physically and spiritually present. The adoration chapel is open 24 hours a day, every single day of the year. In order for it to remain open, there has to be two volunteers present, sentinels, every minute of the year.

Imagine that. If you decided to go to the chapel at 3 in the morning on a Wednesday, you would find two people inside praying.

I volunteered to cover the chapel from 6 to 7 a.m. on Monday mornings. What better way was there to begin my week than to share some quiet time with God? I cherished my hour.

Sometimes I prayed the rosary, sometimes I spent the entire hour thanking God for everything in my life, sometimes I prayed for friends and family, and sometimes I played bible roulette. This is where I would open the bible to any page, read a passage, and reflect on it.

There was always something on any page of the bible that spoke to me. One particular morning, I don't even remember the book or the verse, I could not stop thinking about Haiti. At first I simply thought I was distracted in my prayer, but it kept going back to Haiti. The more I prayed, the more I realized that something needed to be done about the nonexistence of women's health care in Haiti.

Maybe it was up to me to try and get something going. Maybe God was now tapping me on the shoulder.

Later that day, I contacted the Hearts out to Haiti mission at my church, to see if they were interested in doing some type of medical clinic for women. Our church mission is amazing. We sponsor three villages, three parishes, have built several schools, hired teachers, and even sponsor some university students. But their plans were already in place for the coming year and so they passed.

I called my old friend Joe Hurston and asked him for some direction. As usual, he came through. Joe told me about a place called Ruuska Village, just outside the city of Port-au-Prince, where his friend Barbara Walker runs an orphanage and a safe haven for abandoned and abused women. It was perfect.

Then I made a doctor's appointment with Dr. Steve Badolato. You can't run a medical clinic without doctors and I remembered his desire to accompany me on future missions and trips. He came on board immediately and soon we had a team assembled of two doctors, two nurses, my wife and oldest son, and my photographer buddy Craig.

Of course, Joe Hurston came as well. He wanted to see how his protégé would do running his first mission trip.

The mission was a huge success. We ministered to hundreds

of sick women throughout the weekend and spent quality time playing with the orphans. It's amazing how much mileage you can get out of a simple bag of balloons in a third-world country. And though our work there was nothing more than a drop in the bucket of Haiti's problems, filling the leaky old bucket has to start somewhere.

It made me very proud to see my son interact with the children so well. And my wife spent the weekend assisting the doctors, organizing medications, and doing what she does best: caring for and loving the children of the village. I was very proud of both of them, especially how neither complained about "missionary" conditions. I had done it before but was a little worried about them.

We slept on air mattresses in the heat and with the noise of roosters and dogs and crying children. Showers were nothing more than a bucket of well water poured over your body at the end of a long, sweaty, dusty day.

Some of the best, most refreshing showers in my life, have been bucket-baths in Ruuska Village.

It's funny the things you remember. We helped so many people and made so many Haitians happy that weekend by letting them know that the world had not forgotten about them. But the one patient I remember most is the first woman to show up at our makeshift clinic. The one we were unable to help.

She arrived, extremely thin, gaunt, wearing rags for clothing and tiny, worn flip-flops on her feet. She was holding her three-month-old baby in her arms. The mother, we learned, was dying of AIDS. She looked terrible, as if it wouldn't be long now. Her eyes had a sickly, yellowish tinge.

Her baby was being breastfed and had likely contracted the deadly disease as well.

Dr. Steve examined the baby, who had been fussy with bouts of diarrhea. The diagnosis was a simple ear infection and he gave the mother an antibiotic and some fever reducer. When he asked the mother, through a translator, if there was anything else, there was no way we could be prepared for her response.

"I am going to die soon," she said in Creole. "Can you find someone to adopt my baby?"

Steve and I were both stunned. We did not know what to say. The woman trudged away holding her crying baby.

I wrote a front-page story about the mission trip but to this day cannot get that woman or her child out of my mind.

The Schwab execution was stayed after a moratorium was put on executions while the U.S. Supreme Court decided if executions by lethal injection constituted cruel and unusual punishment. Beats the heck out of frying in the electric chair, I thought.

Junny's family was livid. They wanted to see some closure. If you're going to sentence someone to death then why wait so long to carry out the sentence, they argued. Killers, they said, had more rights than the victims or their families.

They had waited 16 years now to see their son's killer punished. Junny Sr. said he wanted to sit in the very first row directly behind the pane of glass that would separate him and Schwab and watch him die.

"I want the last thing that monster sees, to be my face," he'd say. "I want the last thing he hears, to be my voice."

Now I have to say that I had been pro-capital punishment for my entire life. And clearly Mark Dean Schwab was a monster, a predator in the truest sense of the word, and if the death penalty was meant for anyone then it would surely be for him, right?

The moratorium was lifted in early 2008 and a July 1 execution date was set. Schwab's attorneys continued filing appeals but it appeared that the justice system had run its course and there were no more avenues left.

My application to witness the execution was approved by the state and I would be one of 36 people on the other side of the glass when Schwab exhaled his last breath.

During this time I interviewed a Catholic prison chaplain, who had done some work with death row inmates' disease for an unrelated story. After he answered all the questions I had, we discussed our faith and I was surprised to hear that he had once been a staunch supporter of capital punishment.

"But being Catholic means you have to be pro-life, because that's what we believe in," he said. "I realized I was a hypocrite because I was against abortions but I was for executions. Pro-life means pro-life, and that includes all life. It's not up to us to determine who should live and die."

His words had a resounding impact on me because I too was a hypocrite. I could not call myself a Catholic and long for this man's execution, no matter what a monster he was. Still, I was conflicted. I was a father. Could I be truthful and say that I wouldn't want the person responsible for raping and murdering my own child to die?

As the execution date drew near, I began to have terrible nightmares filled with demons and devils and vampires. Every time I looked at the clock after being startled awake from these hellish images the time was always the same: 3 a.m.

I started thinking deeply about Mark Dean Schwab and about the things he did to poor little Junny. I wanted to pray for Schwab as well as Junny but could not bring myself to.

I went to the church to see if I could speak with someone there about the angst I was going through. And it's funny how God works. The day I showed up, all the priests were out doing work: one was at a hospital; one was at a funeral; and another was out of the country. So I told my story, my angst, my dreams to the secretary in the church office.

I told her that I was waking at 3 every morning from these terrible nightmares.

She smiled.

"Do you know what 3 o'clock is?" she asked.

"Yes," I told her. "I know that 3 in the afternoon is when Jesus died."

"Yes, but 3 in the morning is when Jesus looked over at Peter and forgave him for denying him three times. It's the hour of divine mercy."

I've never verified that. I never felt I had to. It was just what I needed to hear: divine mercy. Jesus forgave Peter. God forgave me and welcomed back yet another prodigal son. There is mercy, and there is love for anyone who truly seeks it.

At that moment I was able to start praying for a child-raping killer. I prayed to God every night that Mark Dean Schwab would find his way back to Jesus before it was too late. I prayed that he was truly sorry for what he had done and I even prayed that God would take pity on him.

I maintained close contact with the family, even calling them occasionally just to say hello. But I never told them about the conflicts I had been facing.

The nightmares went away and on the morning of July 1, 2008, I made the four-hour drive to Union Correctional Institution in a town called Starke where all of the state's executions took place. It is a depressing town where it seems like the only place to work is at one of the two maximum security prisons located there.

Despite resolving some of the issues I was dealing with in my head regarding the execution, I was so nervous when they boarded the reporters from the staging area to the inside of the prison that I nearly threw up.

We had learned that Schwab's last meal consisted of breakfast, eggs and sausage with chocolate milk. We also earned that he spent the afternoon having a full contact visit with his mother.

The viewing room and the execution chamber were much smaller than I had imagined. The 36 seats were arranged in three rows, all close together and on the side of the glass there was what looked like a small doctor's examination room.

We were instructed not to speak, not to react, and not to make a sound.

I could see Junny Sr. in the front row, just as he promised. I hoped that he would not start banging on the glass once the execution got under way. I mean, it would have made for one heck of a story to write, but still I hoped he would not do it.

It seemed as if we were in there forever waiting for Schwab to be brought in. It was deathly silent and I decided to close my eyes for a moment and pray. This time I prayed for myself. I prayed that God would shield me from the horror that I was to witness. I prayed that I would make it through. I tried my best to remember Psalm 91 and recite as much of it as I could.

"He who dwells in the shelter of the Most High will rest in the shadow of the Almighty. I will say of the LORD, He is my refuge and my fortress, my God, in whom I trust. Surely he will save you from the fowler's snare and from the deadly pestilence. He will cover you with his feathers, and under his wings you will find refuge; his faithfulness will be your shield and rampart. You will not fear the terror of night, nor the arrow that flies by day, nor the pestilence that stalks in the darkness, nor the plague that destroys at midday. A thousand may fall at your side, ten thousand at your right hand, but it will not come near you," I prayed as best as I could remember.

When I opened my eyes, I saw something remarkable. It looked as if everyone in that room was praying, eyes closed and lips moving slightly.

They wheeled Schwab in and he immediately closed his eyes. He gave no response when the warden asked if he had any final statement to make. The room was deathly quiet and the drugs were administered. The first drug was one to induce deep sleep.

The doctor in the room with him tapped Schwab's eyelids and shook him to make sure he was indeed asleep. Then the poisons were given and Schwab's skin color changed slowly from pink to gray to a tinge of green. His jaw gaped open and in a few minutes he was dead.

It took a few minutes for the doctor to officially make the call. Once he did, Corrections officers opened the door and the 36 of us were let out starting with the front row. Journalists were seated in the back row and I was in the last chair to the left, the one closest to the door.

Everyone had to walk right by me on their way out. Junny stopped when he saw me, put his hand on my shoulder, and said, "Thank you for being here today."

Moments later, at a press conference given by the family, Junny mentioned me several times. I had no idea that my presence there would give him so much comfort but it did.

We embraced and I told him it was finally over.

TEN

IN LATE 2008, I did a series of stories about William Dillon. This was a man who had been convicted of murder in 1981 and sentenced to life in prison. Like many of the prisoners who write to me or who I take the time to go and visit, Dillon maintained his innocence.

But when I started looking into his case, I saw some striking similarities with another couple of Brevard County cases, where men had been wrongfully accused, convicted, and incarcerated. All three cases utilized a former Pennsylvania State Trooper who was working as an expert dog handler and tracker. This man, John Preston, claimed his dogs could do miraculous things. They could detect scents under water. They could track a scent years after a crime had been committed. They could detect a scent through heavy traffic and through homes.

Well, of course, no dog could do things like this and in 1984 he was exposed as a fraud. In fact, the Arizona Supreme Court branded him a "charlatan."

All three cases also used the testimony of jailhouse snitches who gave the state favorable testimony in exchange for reduced sentences or charges.

And all three relied on shaky eyewitness testimony. In Dillon's case, his girlfriend, Donna Parrish, testified that he had committed the murder. The problem was that she was having a sexual relationship with the lead detective in her case.

She recanted her testimony immediately after Dillon was found guilty but the judge did not grant a new trial. Dillon would spend the rest of his life in prison.

When I visited Dillon in prison, I came away with a feeling unlike any before meeting a state prisoner—I actually believed him.

The Innocence Project of Florida, a group that helps exonerate the wrongly convicted through the use of DNA testing, had taken up his cause as well and was fighting the state to allow testing on decades-old evidence left in the case.

Just about the only thing left after all these years was a bloody T-shirt that the state insisted throughout the trial had to have been worn by the killer. Since the murder happened on a hot, humid August night, there could possibly be DNA left on the shirt in the killer's perspiration stains.

DNA was successfully extracted from the shirt and it belonged to a man, a man other than William Dillon. A week before Thanksgiving 2008, the state granted Dillon a new trial and he was released on bond, spending his first night in nearly 28 years outside of a prison cell.

While all this was going on, my family discovered a new and tremendously fun way to get more involved with our parish, the theater ministry! Now I'm not talking about terrible amateur theater or puppet shows or anything like that. No, the Holy Name of Jesus theater group—the HNJ Players—puts on incredible performances of terrific shows in a state of the art theater with professional sound, lighting, and music.

Now, while I am a bit of a ham, I do have a fear of public speaking because I will occasionally fall back into my stuttering. It's not anything that holds me back really, but I'd hate to be onstage in front of 500 paying theater-goers and I start stuttering and stammering. So, I've always joked with my kids that the only shows I would ever try out for would be *A Christmas Carol*, *Les Miserables*, or *Jesus Christ Superstar*.

Well, wouldn't you know it, right there in our church bulletin one Sunday was a casting call for our very own production of Charles Dickens' *A Christmas Carol*.

The entire family auditioned and believe it or not we all got cast. Here's where a bit of Christian humility came in handy, however. Assured that I had nailed my audition for the part of the ghost of Jacob Marley, I could hardly believe it when I was cast in the role of "Old Joe the ragman." In fact, I thought Jennifer was joking when she was on the telephone with the director and I could see her writing "Old Joe."

Of course, the director was right and we had a great time, all of us taking multiple roles in the ensemble production of a sinner's redemption. On the night of the first performance, the director gathered the cast and crew together and gave us some final words of advice.

"Remember what the essence of this story is about," she said. "This is a story about the power of Christ's love and forgiveness."

She was right. They were powerful words and I was thankful to hear them. The economy was starting to tank and several of my close friends at the newspaper had just been laid off. I needed the inspiration.

My wonderful parents drove over from Florida's west coast to see the show and they loved it. There was another special guest that weekend as well: William Dillon.

It was the first live theater show he had ever seen. He hugged me after the performance and admitted that there were several times when he was reduced to tears. But no lines touched him more than when the Ghost of Christmas Present admonishes Scrooge by using the very words the old miser uttered earlier in the show when asked to consider the homeless and the poor.

"Are there no prisons?" the ghost bellowed. "Are there no workhouses? Those who are badly off had better go there."

A few weeks later, the state dropped charges all together and Dillon remains a free man trying to rebuild his life.

Jennifer and I returned to Haiti together a second time and in early February 2009, I organized another medical mission trip, this time to the rural mountain villages of Nicaragua. This tiny Central American country was nothing like Haiti except that the people were also poor. In Haiti there is always the feeling in the back of your mind that the country could erupt in violence or civil war. It's just one of those places that never actually feel completely safe.

I describe Haiti to people as being as close to hell on earth. Everyone is unemployed, there is desperation and hunger everywhere, and there is violence and a very real absence of hope.

Nicaragua was gorgeous and once again the team's main medical doctor was my close friend Steve Badolato. We went to some very small villages near Nueva Guinea, where the people on donkeys far outnumbered the people in cars. The team felt safe and this time I doubled as a journalist writing about the trip for the *Florida Catholic* newspaper and as a translator for the doctors. One day I served as a translator for 60 patients suffering from an array of woes, ranging from erectile dysfunction to asthma to the flu and spots on one man's tongue.

It felt great to be able to utilize my Spanish skills, no matter how poor they are. It didn't matter that I was using words in the wrong tense and struggling through a language that I wish I knew how to speak more fluently. I was able to get the job done. I could understand what the patients were telling me and I could relay to them what the doctors were saying.

The countryside was beautiful and the people living in the tin roof shacks with no television or modern conveniences that we are used to seemed happy and at peace with their lives. They didn't need blackberry cell phones or iPods or 375 satellite television channels to be content.

We took a day off from our work to visit some volcanoes and the views were incredible. We also had time to visit Roberto Clemente Stadium in Managua. Clemente, a Puerto Rican baseball player, was killed delivering earthquake supplies to Nicaragua in 1973. He remains a hero in both places.

Shortly after returning from the trip, I was trying to work off some of my spare tire on the treadmill when I received inspiration from the Holy Spirit to write a stage play. The entire idea, plot, beginning, middle, and end came to me during a 30-minute slow jog. I could hardly wait to get out of the gym and drive home to tell my wife.

The story would focus on the people who had rooms at the inn when Jesus was forced to be born in a manger. The people, six in total, would all have interactions with Jesus later in life. Tying the entire story together would be a narrator who would also be part of the story in a surprise twist at the end.

Jennifer loved it and said it even made the hairs on her neck stand on end.

"How did you come up with that?" she asked.

"I didn't. The Holy Spirit gave it to me."

I started hammering away on my computer keyboard and before I knew it I had written a 90-minue Christmas play. I was pleased with it but the real test would be trying to get someone to produce it.

When I felt it was ready enough for a reading, I contacted some of the wonderful actors I met during *A Christmas Carol* to see if they could read through the lines for director Terry Lynch and our church's music director George Kobosko.

George has final say on things like this and he is not an easy person to please. He is a little picky, which, of course, I understand he has to be. Seeing him there, however, at the reading made me nervous that he would not like it. On the other hand, having him there assured me of at least one honest assessment.

During the reading I could see some of the actors tear up. One man even wiped the tears that were rolling down his face. Just hearing my words come to life was a dream come true. I had written a play and people were actually reading it. This was wonderful that I even was able to stir some emotion. So what if George ends up hating it. At least I will have had this moment.

The second we were done, George whipped out a calendar book and started looking at December dates to make sure the theater would be free. He called the play profound and moving.

"We have to put this play on," he said to my utter amazement.

About this time, I wrote a story about a little girl from Haiti, actually from Barbara's Ruuska Village, who had suffered extreme burns on her left arm. The wounds went untreated in Haiti and her mother abandoned her at the orphanage saying she could no longer care for her.

The arm had atrophied and was basically unusable. The scar tissue continued to harden and would soon choke the arm completely dead. In all likelihood it would have to be amputated. In Haiti, that could be a death sentence.

Dr. Steve Badolato arranged for the little girl, Lensa, to fly into Brevard County on a medical visa and he lined up a team of orthopedic surgeons and plastic surgery specialists to help make Lensa as whole as they could.

She would never fully regain use of her arm but now she might be able to have hope.

She underwent four surgeries.

I was moved by Steve's compassion for the girl and impressed by how quickly he was able to orchestrate her care.

My play, meanwhile, was in production and we had started rehearsals. But as I know from experience, the devil hates to see good things in Christ succeed, we started having problems. The director had a family emergency and was forced to leave for several weeks. One of the actors became ill and dropped out. And another actor's 43-year-old nephew suddenly dropped dead of a heart attack forcing him to leave town. It seemed as if the play was in jeopardy.

I pulled the crew together and told them how I felt. I told them that I believed this play was going to inspire people. It was going to bring home the Christmas message and really put "Christ" back into Christmas for a lot of people. I told them we needed to believe in this project. I told them we needed to really pull together. I told them we needed to pray.

So at the start of every rehearsal, meeting, or scene production sessions we opened with a prayer. And it became this wonderful time to look forward to when someone new would step forward each night and lead us in praise and worship.

A few weeks before the show opened, I was with my youngest daughter at the soccer field. As I was rushing to get there on time, I saw Steve holding hands with a little girl with a familiar face. It was Lensa.

"Steve, is, is that Lensa?" I asked dumbfounded, assuming that she had been sent back to Barbara's orphanage after receiving the medical care months ago.

"Yep, that's her all right. We're adopting her."

I called Joe Hurston to tell him the news and, well, Joe is an emotional guy and he started weeping on the phone. But it was more, it was deeper than just the usual few tears of joy that we liked to share.

"John, do you realize how this all started?" Joe laughed and cried at the same time. "Do you have any idea of the reverberations of this all?"

I shook my head no on the other end of the telephone but was at a loss for words.

"John, all this is because God tapped some old, tired judge, some old, tired ex-fighter pilot on the shoulder."

And then it all flashed in front of me like the last climactic scene of a movie when the mystery gets solved. If God had not tapped the judge on the shoulder, he would never have called Joe Hurston to get back into mission work. Joe Hurston would have never called me and urged me to drive to Miami to get a passport. I never would have met Robert Bland at Joe Hurston's party and I never would have gone to Africa.

If I never went to Africa then I would not have seen Jesus when I did and I would not have gone back to the church. I never would have reconnected with Dr. Badolato and he never would have started going on medical mission trips with me. He never would have heard of Ruuska Village and would never have arranged for the little girl with the withered arm to come to the states.

She would never have been adopted.

Throw in all the stories I wrote and the money they raised for relief efforts. Throw in all the water purifiers Joe deployed around the globe. Think of how many thousands of people were now drinking clean water.

I felt dizzy.

"John, because God tapped the judge on the shoulder, thousands of people have been touched. Thousands, do you hear me? Thousands because of that one little tap."

The play was a huge success. It was one of the proudest moments of my life to see the reaction my words had on the audience and cast alike. Our pastor, Father David Page, always makes it a point to attend the last performance the HNJ Players put on. Maybe he knows that by then all the kinks will have been worked out.

In any event, he likes to take the microphone when it is all said and done to thank the cast as well as the patrons. This theater ministry is terrific in that it raises money for church programs, entertains, and sometimes even evangelizes.

No matter how large or small a role you had in a production, it always feels great to hear Father Page acknowledge the hard work and effort. But little could prepare me for the accolades he would bestow on me.

"I came here today expecting the usual sort of Christmas pageant, centered on the birth of Jesus," he began. "Instead, what I received was the most powerful of sermons incorporating all four gospels, the kind of sermon I know many priests and deacons wish they could write."

The cast pushed me forward and the crowd responded with a standing ovation. I cried tears of joy and appreciation.

"But I'm not surprised," Father Page continued, "because John is a man who lives the gospel."

Then he went through the mission trips I organized and the stories I had written. I don't think I will ever feel as proud and as humbled as I did at that very moment. It was a terrific kickoff to a wonderful Christmas season.

My sister Nancy, her husband Jason, and their son Logan visited from Michigan. We brought in the New Year at my parent's home and it rekindled so many of the good memories I had growing up.

Seeing my parents dote on Isabelle and Logan made me realize how much they loved us kids. Everyone has faults. No one is perfect. Father Tony at church always reminds us that church is a hospital for sinners, not a museum of saints.

Maybe what matters most is how you finish this thing, the amount of love that pours through when it's all said and done.

Do I forgive my parents? I've never needed to. They did their best and I couldn't love two people anymore than I love them.

As 2009 drew to an end, there seemed to be a slight upturn in the economy, giving hope to those of us leery that the newspaper would shut down. That being said, we were forced to take an unpaid week of absence, a furlough, during the first quarter of 2010.

Since I was on vacation for the last week of 2009, I decided to take my furlough during the first week of the year, giving me a two-week holiday. But during the last few days of my furlough, I came down with the flu. So, I might be the only Gannett employee to ever have used the trifecta of vacation, furlough, and two sick days consecutively.

I was feeling slightly better that Tuesday evening and was planning on making it back to the office Wednesday morning.

It never happened.

Shortly before 6 p.m. I noticed a missed phone call on my cell phone from my mother-in-law. She left a tearful message about a terrible earthquake in Haiti.

I switched on the television and was amazed that Haiti was actually the lead story on several 24-hour news stations. Haiti? Seriously? No one cared about Haiti, this one must be really serious.

I watched for a while but images were sparse. I heard words like catastrophic, historic, and tragic. Still groggy from the flu, it took a few minutes to sink in.

Then, I called Joe Hurston.

"This is bad, John," he said. "I'm leaving at 4 in the morning. There's room on the plane if you want to go."

As if able to hear the conversation, or just from knowing that Joe always has room on his plane for me, Jennifer started nodding yes, you need to go, this is Haiti. She was hooked as desperately as I was to help these sweet-natured people in this impoverished nation. Nothing ever seems to miss Haiti—earthquakes, hurricanes, tropical storms, mudslides, disease—you name it and it will eventually hit this tiny country dead on.

I called the newspaper and started making promises I wasn't sure I could keep.

"I'll file lots of stories, send back tons of photos, and I'll even blog and twitter," I boasted.

But the truth was that there was no way of knowing what Haiti's infrastructure was like and what I would be able to do. But I knew that I needed to go.

Our plan was for the small team Joe had assembled to meet in Titusville at 4 a.m. so we could be in the air by 5 a.m. But God had a different plan.

I made the one-hour drive north to Titusville after the obligatory trip to Walmart for supplies. Having traveled to numerous disaster sites and third-world countries I consider myself an expert at knowing what to pack. For this trip I would be packing light, though I didn't know how long we would be there.

I bought hand sanitizer, wet wipes, granola bars, beef jerky, and ear plugs. If I could only pack one item on a trip like this it would definitely be wet wipes. The most important thing is having clean privates and clean feet. Everything else can go for a few days.

I pulled into the lot and I could see Joe wearing a slight frown, his face looking slightly tighter and more intense than usual. Doug, the guy who took back some of the sadness from the tsunami in Indonesia with me, was supposed to be flying us in his plane but had called Joe only moments earlier.

Doug had dutifully and correctly fueled his plane the night before. But when he returned that morning, there were sixty gallons of fuel spilled out onto the tarmac. The plane had a fuel leak.

But instead of giving up and sending everyone back home, Joe instructed us to caravan down to Stuart—roughly a two-hour drive—for another plane.

The plan was to drive down to Marlin Moudy's home, knock on his door at 6 a.m., and beg him to fly us to Haiti.

That's what Joe's faith is like.

The sad truth about Haiti is that from the sky over Port-au-Prince, it was impossible to tell what was earthquake damage and what was previously existing ruins and slums. The airport was closed and the air traffic tower abandoned. We all peered out of the tiny windows of the six-seater plane to make sure no other planes were trying to land at the same time we were.

I ran into Al Roker on the tarmac.

We landed in Haiti 19 hours after the earthquake that killed hundreds of thousands.

By the time we got past the military and out into Barbara Walker's waiting truck, it was dark and impossible to see the damage. What was visible, however, was the stunned, dazed look on just about everyone's face.

Less than one day earlier the ground shook violently for 30 seconds, sending the majority of the capital's buildings toppling down or crumbling. They were shell-shocked. The streets were filled with people, wandering with no apparent destinations and not even talking to each other.

We stayed in Barbara's village and incredibly her high-speed wireless Internet was working as well as her phone lines. I sent the paper a short story and a photo before crashing for the night.

I slept outdoors on an air mattress, using my rolled-up jeans as a pillow. The roosters cried all night long as well as many of the villagers, who were sleeping outdoors too. I did not want to die beneath a heap of Haitian building rubble.

I experienced my first tremor when I was thrown clear of the air mattress in the middle of the night. I stood up and braced for another that never came. I went back to sleep. In the morning I was reminded of something I forgot to pack: bug spray. My arms and face were covered with about 50 mosquito bites.

Before going to assess the damage in the capital, Joe needed to get some of his water purifiers up and running. I wandered around the village and was shocked by the earthquake's reach, even here, eight miles from the epicenter. Every single building, house, shed, structure, retaining wall was damaged. Some had pancaked straight down, others were leaning and others were cracked.

I took a short walk and came upon a man sifting through the rubble of what used to be his house as his ducks and chickens pecked at the ground nearby. The collection of things he had saved made me a bit sad. There was a suit, probably for funerals, some brightly colored plastic food containers, and a few pots and pans. Everything else was gone.

I asked him to describe what happened and he explained he ran from his house and watched as it came down. He didn't know whether it was an earthquake or an explosion of some sort. With no FEMA, government aid, or any type of insurance I wondered how this man would continue. I mean, how on earth do you start starting over? Where do you sleep? What do you eat? How long would it take to clear away the rubble? How long would it be before he had a roof over his head?

Would his life ever get back to normal?

I asked him if he was bitter or angry but he gave me a look like I was crazy.

"I am so happy because God spared my life," he said. "So many people are dead but God spared me. I am lucky."

Then he turned his head quickly as if he heard something beneath the rubble. He dropped to his knees and started digging with his hands. I snapped photo after photo as he pulled and tossed pieces of concrete to the side. Then a wide grin came over his face. He reached down further, laying his body down on the ground to get his hand down deeper.

He started laughing out loud as he pulled up one of his ducks, slightly frightened but none worse for wear really. He held the duck up high and kissed it on the back. Then he carefully placed it on the ground.

That was one lucky duck and one very blessed man to have the attitude that he did.

Hundreds of thousands of others were not nearly as lucky. During the next few days I toured the tent cities that were popping up everywhere, checked on other missions, and forced myself to tour the hardest hit areas of the city. As a journalist I knew it was something I had to do, but I also knew that I would be putting images into my head that I might never be able to extinguish.

I was right.

The city that used to be Port-au-Prince was in complete ruins and chaos. There were fires everywhere; the air was filled with smoke and the stench of death. Cars were upside down or lying flattened beneath parts of buildings. Every government building was gone. The prison was in shambles and the inmates running free.

The smell of death was everywhere and the flies were multiplying by the millions. They were all over, landing on your skin, on your food. The knowledge that they had just been feasting on the dead was enough to make you wretch.

I described walking in tsunami-torn Indonesia as being on the set of a science-fiction disaster movie. But there was no comparison visually. In Indonesia it was as if the water came in and took everything out to sea. But Port-au-Prince looked like a post-apocalyptic movie set. This was hell.

There was no way this city was ever going to recover from this disaster.

And I'm not sure if there is any way I will recover from seeing all the bodies. They lined the city streets, they were on corners amid the trash, and they were piled outside the morgue. They were everywhere, bloated, frozen in position, arms outstretched as if to stop the falling debris.

There were bodies in the courtyard of a small hospital where surgeons inside performed one amputation after another in order to save lives. I thought the dead in the courtyard were covered in black sheets. But when I saw the sheets moving about, I stepped closer to see. The bodies were black with buzzing flies.

The first night I lay for hours unable to sleep. I cried for these mothers, fathers, children, brothers, and sisters whose bodies were forced to rot out in the sun, whose lives were cut short in such a terrifying way. I tried listening to music on my iPod to help me sleep but it did not work. Only when I prayed was I able to find peace enough to sleep.

I can still see them when I close my eyes and lay my head down at night.

And the poor Haitian people could do nothing but eventually go on with their lives as if the bodies were not laying 10 feet away.

There was very little I could do but report the story and try to keep this terrible disaster in the news for as long as the American people could stomach it. But I guess that's what I do. Joe saves lives by providing clean water. Dr. Steve saves lives with his medical knowledge. There was little else I could do except write, take photos, spread the word, and pray.

But sometimes that's enough.

I remember walking through a tent city. Actually the word "tent" is really a gross overstatement. These tents were made up of a couple of sticks propped together with a blanket, a rag, or an old towel draped over the top. But I was walking through and I was struck by the sight of a woman, probably about 60 years old, who was sitting on a pile of rubble and twisted metal that used to be her home. She was wearing a dress and her hair was pulled back very tightly into a bun.

She sat there with back arched in perfect posture reading a copy of the New Testament.

I was taken aback. There was chaos and noise and despair all around her and she was reading the good news. I walked over to her with my translator and her story was very much like the rest: house ruined, relatives dead, nowhere to go, and no means to start over.

"Everything is gone," she said through the translator, holding up her book. "The only thing I have left is Jesus."

A crowd of Haitians had gathered around us now curious as to what I was doing. I took her by the arm and did the only thing I could.

"He will always be faithful," I told her, surprised that I was capable of evangelizing. "He will never abandon you."

She thanked me, shook my hand, and broke down crying. God had used me in that moment to give strength, encouragement, and even hope to someone who desperately needed it.

I made two trips to Haiti in the three weeks following the earthquake. The second was to accompany a group of doctors assembled in part by Dr. Steve, who volunteered at just about the only functioning hospital in Port-au-Prince. Both times I knew that part of my mission was to take some of the sadness back with me.

ON HIGHER GROUND

Driving home from Stuart after my first trip in mid-January, I fell asleep at the wheel doing 75 miles per hour on I-95 North. I woke to the sound of the car rattling and shaking uncontrollably on the grassy median only yards away from oncoming traffic.

I slammed the brakes, turned the wheel, and my Nissan Sentra started spinning. I don't know how many times it went completely around but I could feel the vehicle wanting to flip. I came to a complete stop facing the wrong way on the interstate, stalled.

There were no cars.

I backed up onto the shoulder and sat there for a moment, my hands frozen to the wheel and my heart crashing into the walls of my chest. I knew I should have been dead. It was as if the hand of God had reached down and shielded my car from the wreckage. It even started right up. I thanked Jesus out loud and for the rest of the 75 minutes left in my journey home, His precious name graced my lips.

I should have been dead, but God did not allow it.

No, He has more plans in store for me. There must be things He wants me to do. I'm sure there must be many more journeys and adventures ahead, just as there are for all of us. Sometimes we don't recognize it or are scared to answer the call.

Don't worry if you don't recognize it right away.

He never gives up. Trust me, I know.

www.ingramcontent.com/pod-product-compliance
Lightning Source LLC
Chambersburg PA
CBHW031250290426
44109CB00012B/518